THINGS MY SON NEEDS TO KNOW ABOUT THE WORLD

This Large Print Book carries the
Seal of Approval of N.A.V.H.

Things My Son Needs to Know About the World

Fredrik Backman

Translated by Alice Menzies

THORNDIKE PRESS
A part of Gale, a Cengage Company

Farmington Hills, Mich • San Francisco • New York • Waterville, Maine
Meriden, Conn • Mason, Ohio • Chicago

LIBRARY OF CONGRESS CIP DATA ON FILE.
CATALOGUING IN PUBLICATION FOR THIS BOOK
IS AVAILABLE FROM THE LIBRARY OF CONGRESS

ISBN-13: 978-1-4328-6717-1 (hardcover alk. paper)

Published in 2019 by arrangement with Atria Books, an imprint of Simon & Schuster, Inc.

Printed in Mexico
1 2 3 4 5 6 7 23 22 21 20 19

Son,

*This book is dedicated
to your grandmother,
because she taught me to love words.*

*And to you,
for all those other reasons.*

CONTENTS

To my son:

I want to apologize.

For everything I'm going to do over the next eighteen or so years. For everything I'll miss. Everything I won't understand. All the notes about parent-teacher conferences you won't want to show me.

For all the times I'll embarrass you. All the camps and field trips I'll volunteer myself to. All the girlfriends or boyfriends you'll never want to bring home for dinner.

For doing my mom-was-wrong-and-dad-was-right dance around other people.

For that time when your school invites all the parents to a softball tournament and I take it a bit too seriously. For calling your math teacher "a frikkin' flathead!" For trying to high-five your friends.

For buying a minivan.

For wearing shorts.

For being late the first time you're invited

to a real birthday party. For being pissed when there are lines for the rides at the amusement park. For calling the assistant in the skateboard shop "man." For not understanding that you would rather do gymnastics than play soccer. For all the times I forget to lock the bathroom door — what is seen can't be unseen.

For the holidays. The cowboy hat. The REAL MEN WEIGH OVER 200 POUNDS T-shirt. The speech at your high school graduation party.

For all the times I get a bit drunk and start telling the joke about the two Irishmen in a boat again. I really, really want to apologize for all those things.

But when you're the most angry at me, I want you to try to remember that, to me, you'll always be the tiny one-year-old boy standing naked in the hallway with a toothless grin and a cuddly lion clutched to your chest.

Whenever I'm difficult. Whenever I'm embarrassing. Unreasonable. Unfair. I want you to think back to that day.

That day when you refused to tell me where the hell you'd hidden my damn car keys. And I want you to remember that it was *you* who started it.

Your Dad

What You Need to Know About Motion-Sensitive Bathroom Lights

So. I'm the one who's your dad. I know you've started to understand that now. Up until now, you've really just sailed through life and let the rest of us do all the hard work. But as far as I've been told, you're now one and a half, and that's the age when you can start learning things. Tricks. That kind of stuff. I'm very positive about that, let me tell you right now.

Because I want you to understand that this whole parenthood thing isn't as easy as it looks. There's a hell of a lot to keep track of. Diaper bags. Car seats. Nursery rhymes. Extra socks. Poop. Above all, poop. There's a *lot* of poop to keep track of. It's nothing personal. You can ask any parent with small children. That whole first year, jeez, your entire life revolves around poop.

The presence of poop. The absence of poop. The discovery of poop. The aromatic sensation of poop. The waiting for poop.

13

Seriously, I can't express how much of your life will be spent waiting for poop once you have children.

"Shall we go? Okay! Has it happened yet? Huh? What did you say? It hasn't? Damn it. Okayokayokay. Stay calm, no need to panic. What time is it? Should we wait for it? Or do we go now and hope we make it there before it? Let's risk it! Okay! Not okay? What if it happens on the way? You're right. Okay. Quiet, so I can think! Okay, but what if we wait here and then nothing happens, then what do we do? Risk it and go anyway? And then if it happens on the way and we're like, 'God. Damn. Sonofa . . . BIKE! If we'd just left straightaway instead of arguing about it, we would've made it there before the poop!!!' "

You get it? That's what it's like all the time once you've reproduced. Your entire life revolves around the logistics of poop. You start having discussions about it with strangers, all matter-of-factly. The consistency, the color, the departure schedule. Poop on your fingers. Poop on your clothes. Poop that gets stuck in the cracks between the tiles on the bathroom floor. You start talking about the metaphysical experience of poop. Breaking it down to the academic level. When those Swiss physicists appeared in the media a couple of years ago talking about their groundbreaking research and the discovery of a "previously unknown particle" that could travel faster than the speed of light, and the entire world was wondering what this new particle might consist of, all parents with small children looked at one another in unison and just said: "Poop. I bet anything it's poop."

And the worst thing isn't even the poop itself. The worst is the moments of not knowing. When you see those small twitches on your baby's face and say, "Was that . . . ? It looked like she . . . but maybe she was making a grimace? Maybe she just . . . farted? Oh God, we have three more hours to go of this airplane ride, please tell me it was just a fart!" And then you have to wait those five seconds. They're the longest five seconds in the history of the universe, I can guarantee you that. There are ten thousand eternities and a life-affirming French drama between each of them. And then, finally, as though it were one of those scenes in *The Matrix* where time itself slows down, the scent reaches your nostrils. And it's like being hit in the face with a sack of wet concrete. The walk to the airplane bathroom after that, it's like when the warring slaves marched out to battle the lions in the Colosseum. I swear, when you come back out afterward you feel like those warriors must have felt when they returned to Rome after beating the barbarians, but on the way in you are known by only one name: Gladiator.

When you're older, I'll tell you about the very first poop. The ancient, eternal, original poop. The one all babies poop at some point during the twenty-four hours after birth. It's completely black. Like evil itself had pooped. No joke.

Changing that diaper was my Vietnam.

And sure, you might be wondering why I'm bringing this up now. But I just want you to know how everything in life hangs together. Poop is part of the world, you see. And right now, when issues around the environment and sustainable development are so important, you need to understand the part that poop plays in the grand scheme of things. The importance poop has had for modern technology.

Because, you know, the world hasn't always been like this. There was a time before everything was electronics and computers. Can you believe that when I was young, if you watched a film and couldn't remember an actor's name, there was no way for you to find out! You had to wait until the next day and then go to the library to look it up. I know. Sick. Or you would have to call a friend to ask, but then get your head around this: if you did that, you might have to hang up after ten rings and say, "Nah, he's not home." Not *h-o-m-e,* can you imagine that?

It was a different time. But then all this technology came along. The Internet and mobile phones and touch screens and all that crap, and it just put a *huge* amount of pressure on my generation when we became parents, you know? Every other generation of parents could just say they "didn't know." That's what our parents do. Drank wine while you were breast-feeding? "Didn't know." Let us eat cinnamon buns for breakfast? "Didn't know." Put us in the back seat without a seat belt? Took just a little bit of LSD while you were pregnant? "Please, we didn't *k-n-o-w.* It was the seventies, you know. LSD wasn't dangerous back then!"

But my generation knows, OKAY? We know EVERYTHING! So if anything goes sideways with your childhood, I'll be held responsible. It will never be legally sustainable that I acted "in good faith." I could have googled it. I should have googled it. My God, why didn't I google it?

Damn it.

We just don't want to make mistakes. That's all. We're an entire generation who grew up and became specialists in one or two things. We have Web shops and tax deductions and consultants and personal trainers and Apple Support. We don't do trial and error; we call someone who knows. Nature didn't prepare us for you.

So we google things. We read online forums. We call the medical advice line because you *almost* hit your head on the corner of a table, just to ask whether it could cause "psychological damage," because we don't want to risk you failing trigonometry when you're sixteen and then thinking, "Maybe he suffered post-traumatic stress? Is that why?" We don't want to be held responsible for the fact that you were out all night playing with your stupid laser weapons and hovercrafts instead of studying.

Because we love you.

That's all this is about. We want you to be better than us. Because if our kids don't grow up to be better than us, then what's the point of all this? We want you to be kinder, smarter, more humble, more generous, and more selfless than we are. We want to give you the very best circumstances we can possibly provide. So we follow sleeping methods and go to seminars and buy ergonomic bathtubs and push car-seat salesmen up against the wall and shout, "The safest! I want THE SAFEST, doyouhearme?!" (Not that I've ever done that, of course; you shouldn't pay so much attention to what your mother says.)

We keep your entire childhood electronically monitored to such a degree that it makes the *Big Brother* house look like a damn wonder of integrity, and we go to baby swim lessons and buy breathable, practical clothing in gender-neutral colors and we're just so insanely, insanely terrified of making a mistake. So indescribably scared of not being good enough. Because we spent so long being the biggest narcissists in world history before we became parents and realized how unimportant we really were.

The realization that you will, from that moment on, draw all your breaths through someone else's lungs hits you harder when you aren't prepared.

And all we want is to protect you. To save you from life's disappointments and shortcomings and unhappy romances. We actually haven't got a clue what we're really doing — having kids is in many ways like trying to drive a bulldozer through a china shop. With broken legs. Wearing a back-to-front ski mask. While drunk.

But we're going to try, damn it. Because we want to be the best parents we ever could be. That's all.

So we google things. We google everything. And we care about the environment. Because we didn't inherit the Earth from our parents, we're borrowing it from our children and all that crap. We believe in that crap! We're ready to fight for that crap! We have framed posters with sunsets and rocks and really inspirational quotes and crap on them on our living room walls and everything! We buy better cars. We recycle. We install small motion sensors on all our lights so that they automatically go out when there's no one in the room. And sometimes, we take things a step too far. We do it with the very best of intentions, but sometimes we just want too much. Sometimes, my generation is just so incredibly overambitious, please try to understand that. And that's when some bloody genius decides to install those motion sensors in the restroom with the baby-changing facilities at the shopping center. So that the lights go out after we've been in there for thirty seconds.

So, here we are. You and I. And the poop. In the dark.

You're not old enough to have seen gymnasts competing hanging in those wooden ring things in the Olympics, but that's roughly what it looks like when the lights go out while I'm sitting on the toilet myself and need to try to turn them on again. So you can just imagine the modern interpretation of *Swan Lake* it takes to be able to turn them back on when you have a diaper as heavy as a dumbbell in one hand and half a pack of moist wipes in the other, standing on one leg to stop your baby from falling off the changing table with one knee.

And it's right then, at that very moment, that I feel like my generation might have taken the whole environmentally friendly technology thing just a small step too far. That's just how I feel. Get it?

I think you get it.

I just want you to know that I love you. Once you're older, you'll realize that I made an endless line of mistakes during your childhood. I know that. I've resigned myself to it. But I just want you to know that I did my very, very best. I left it all on the field. I gave this every ounce of everything I had.

I googled like hell.

But it was really, really, really dark in there. And there was poop . . . everywhere. Sometimes, you just have to follow your gut.

Honestly, you should be happy we even got out of there alive.

If I Die, never Forget This.

1. Jump off the roller coaster.
2. Grab the hanging rope, wait until you get to the ship, and then take the keg of rum.
3. Grab the flask of oil from the lamp.
4. Use the oil with the rope, and the rope with the keg of rum. Go to the big snow monkey and put the keg of rum under the snow monkey's arm.
5. When LeChuck turns up and tries to burn you, use the pepper on him so that he sneezes on the rope. It will catch fire, the keg of rum will explode, and LeChuck will die.

And *that* is how you complete the final level of Monkey Island 3.

Your mother can roll her eyes all she wants. I am not risking this knowledge dying with my generation.

WHAT YOU NEED TO KNOW ABOUT MY EXPECTATIONS OF YOU

YOUR MOTHER: (*reading a book by a Belgian child psychologist*) It says something here about him being in a developmental phase right now where his brain focuses on very specific brain functions.

ME: All right . . .

YOUR MOTHER: And it says that different children focus on different things. Some children roll around, others develop their verbal abilities, some learn to grip things extremely early . . .

ME: What? You mean different kids get different superpowers?

YOUR MOTHER: (*Doesn't really look like you can put it like that at all*) Yeah . . . sure . . . I guess you could . . . put it like that.

ME: So it's like the Xavier Institute in X-Men?

YOUR MOTHER: (*Sighing*) Yes. Sure. Just like that. If you count "rolling around" as a superpower, that is.

ME: (*Looking at you, lying asleep on a huge cushion on the floor*) Wonder what his superpower is.

YOUR MOTHER: (*Looking at you*) There's no denying he's extremely good at sleeping.

(*Silence*)

ME: Not exactly a SUPER superpower, is it?

YOUR MOTHER: No.

(*Silence*)

ME: He's really just one big disappointment, this kid.

YOUR MOTHER: Hey! You can't say that!

ME: What? You have to admit that the guy who "sleeps well" would've been badly bullied in the X-Men gang.

YOUR MOTHER: (*Picking you up. Leaving the room.*) I'm going to put him to bed so he doesn't have to listen to this.

ME: Do you think Wolverine's mother spoiled him like that? Huh?

(*Silence*)

ME: But now that I'm thinking about it, do you think maybe he's just tired from being OUT ALL NIGHT FIGHTING EVIL?

THE MATHEMATICS OF BIRTH

NURSE: Aha, and I see here that your little son was born a few weeks early.

ME: Yes, that's right. Week thirty-seven.

NURSE: Well, you see, nooo, it says thirty-six plus five here.

ME: Yes, thirty-six weeks and five days. That's surely the thirty-seventh week?

NURSE: Well, you see, nooo, we don't count it that way, you see. We have him down as thirty-six plus five.

ME: So . . . you're saying he was born in the thirty-sixth week, then?

NURSE: Thirty-six plus five, yes.

ME: But surely that's the thirty-seventh week?

NURSE: Well, you see, nooo . . . we don't count it that way, you see.

ME: What do you mean "don't count it that way." You count weeks, don't you?

NURSE: Well, you see, nooo, we count days.

ME: And what the hell do you think weeks consist of?

NURSE: Well, they consist of days. I know that.

ME: So thirty-six weeks, then?

NURSE: Plus five.

ME: So the thirty-sixth week, then?

NURSE: Well. You see. Yeees. Plus five.

ME: But if thirty-six weeks have passed, plus

five days, that surely means it's the thirty-seventh week.

NURSE: Well. Maybe you could look at it that way.

ME: Exactly!

NURSE: But we don't count it like that.

ME: So which week WAS it, then???

NURSE: Thirty-six. Plus five.

ME: So the thirty-sixth week, then?

NURSE: Well, you see . . .

(*Long silence*)

NURSE: What are you looking for?

ME: Painkillers.

NOTE TO SELF

The nurses really don't like it when you use the word "housetrain" in relation to children.

■ ■ ■ ■

WHAT YOU NEED
TO KNOW ABOUT
IKEA

■ ■ ■ ■

Don't pee in the ball pool.

That's really the only advice I can give you.

And don't go against the direction of the arrows painted on the floor. Seriously. I love you and all that, so I'll tell you right now, if you try to go against the direction of the arrows painted on the floor in IKEA, it's every man for himself. There are arrows on the floor, everyone knows that, they show us which way to go, and they're there to prevent anarchy. If everyone wasn't going in the same direction inside IKEA, there would be chaos, do you understand that? Civilization as we know it would collapse into a furious Judgment Day inferno of shadows and fire.

It's not that people will just glare at you and clench their fists in their pockets if you do it, either. IKEA has the least passive passive-aggressive customers in the entire universe. Late-middle-aged women with purple hair and a scent of menthol tobacco will ram your shins with their trolleys like they were industrial whale catchers and you were a rubber boat bearing the Greenpeace logo. Older men will yell swear words/body parts combinations at you. Fathers carrying small children in BabyBjörns will "accidentally" head butt you. Honestly: you could drive the wrong way down the highway and experience less hostility from strangers. You're an outlaw. And I don't mean that in a fun "living in the forest with my friends" kind of way. I mean it's hunting season and you're the prey. I mean that if you were in any of the Robin Hood films and you said, "I'm an outlaw too, can I tag along?" to Kevin Costner and Russell Crowe, they would be all, "What did you say you did? Seriously? Look, man, we've murdered and desecrated and plundered, and we don't mean to moralize or anything, but what the hell is wrong with you? Didn't you see the arrows?!" It's a crime as bad as stealing someone else's parking space. Anyone can kill you after that. Them's the rules.

But otherwise: don't pee in the ball pool. That's really the most important thing.

And yes. I know you might be thinking

that it's strange for me to spend so much time talking about IKEA. Entirely justified. But some of the WORST days of my life have been spent in that place. Truly, other than the dentist and the crematorium, there are no other places I would be prepared to do as much to avoid going to. I mean, I wouldn't chop off an arm or eat excrement or anything, I wouldn't do that. I'm not a lunatic. But on Sundays a few years ago, I seriously might have done anything below that category. For example, your mother once called my bluff and said, "ANY-THING?" and I said, "ANYTHING EX-CEPT IKEA!!!" and then she made me take out the trash naked. But that's another story. But, you know. Then you grow up. You will too. And you'll start to realize other things. Like the fact that some of the very best days of your life will be spent in IKEA too. And that, after a while, the contents of the trunk become meaningless in compari-son to the contents of the passenger seat.

You'll grow up. Leave school. Come home one day and announce that you're not go-ing to university because you're starting a band. Or opening a bar. Or a surf shop in Thailand. You'll pierce your eyebrow and get a tattoo of a dragon on your arse or whatever and start reading books about practical philosophy. And that's fine. It's okay to be an idiot while you're a teenager. It's a teenager's job. But, you know, it's also going to be around that time that I'll tell you that it would probably be a good idea if you moved to your own place. And it won't be anything personal, I want to say that right here and now. It's just that I'll need your room, because I won't have anywhere to put my new pool table otherwise.

And then we'll go to IKEA to buy cutlery and potato peelers and lightbulbs for you. Because that's a parent's job.

I left home in the late nineties. I guess you'll be doing it in the late twenties. The best advice I can give you is to buy enough plates so that you don't have to do the dishes very often. And to have plenty of hidden storage solutions for empty soda cans. And not to keep drugs at home. Yes, I know what you're thinking — you think you'll get away with the whole "they belong to a friend" excuse. But you can forget about your mother believing that when she comes to visit. She's not stupid. She'll know you drank all that soda yourself.

Other than that, I don't want to butt in. A man's first apartment is his own. Though if I were going to give you one tiny bit of advice, it would be to buy your first sofa secondhand. Not from IKEA. Buy one of those brown leather monstrosities as big as the Death Star. The kind you need a minute to be able to classify with certainty as a sofa rather than a bouncy castle. Where the cushions are so worn that they'll smother the fire themselves when your friend Sock falls asleep with a cigarette in his mouth. The kind you'll spend 80 percent of your nights on because it's just not worth the effort of going all the way to bed once you've turned off the video games. Let function come before form. Buy the sofa you want, not the sofa you need. Trust me. You'll never get the chance again.

Because sooner or later, you'll fall in love. And from then on, every sofa you own will be one long compromise. So live while you're young. Spend as much time on the sofa of your dreams as you can.

And I know what you're thinking, you're thinking that a sofa like that will be far too expensive for you. But don't worry. You can get one for free if you agree to go and pick it up.

You might not realize it now, but one day you're going to move in with someone you love too, and by then all this will all be crystal clear.

The majority of things in life are about

picking your battles. You'll learn that too. And that will never be clearer than when you're at IKEA. You'd have to visit a Danish vacation village after two weeks of pouring rain and no beer to come across as many couples arguing as you'll hear in the IKEA section for changeable sofa covers on any given Tuesday. People take this whole interior design thing really seriously these days. It's become a national pastime to overinterpret the symbolism of the fact that "he wants frosted glass, that just proves he never *l-i-s-t-e-n-s* to my FEELINGS." "Ahhhhh! She wants beech veneer. Do you hear me? Beech veneer! Sometimes, it feels like I've woken up next to a stranger!" That's how it is, every single time you go there. And I'm not going to lecture you, but if there's just one thing I can get across then let it be this: no one has ever, in the history of the world, had an argument in IKEA that really is about IKEA. People can say whatever they like, but when a couple who has been married for ten years walks around the bookshelves section calling one another words normally only used by alcoholic crime fiction detectives, they might be arguing about a number of things, but trust me: cupboard doors is not one of them.

Believe me. You're a Backman. Regardless

of how many shortcomings the person you fall in love with might have, I can guarantee that you still come out on top of that bargain. So find someone who doesn't love you for the person you are, but despite the person you are. And when you're standing there, in the storage section at IKEA, don't focus too much on the furniture. Focus on the fact that you've actually found someone who can see themselves storing their crap in the same place as your crap. Because, hand on heart: you have a lot of crap.

In May 2008, I went to an IKEA just outside of Stockholm. It was a Sunday and roughly six thousand degrees and the air-conditioning was broken. Manchester United won the league that day and I missed their last game. Everything but the lemon-flavored sparkling water had run out in the café. An old woman who smelled like cheap cigarettes rammed her trolley into my shins. I was holding the most butt-ugly hallway light I'd ever seen in my arms.

It was one of the happiest days of my life.

The next morning, we signed the lease for our first apartment together. Your first home. People sometimes ask me how I lived before I met your mother. I answer that I didn't.

I wish you nothing less than that.

Even when it means that you too one day will have to give away that brown leather sofa to some nineteen-year-old moron in an Arsenal shirt who comes over to your place with a Jägermeister-smelling friend one Saturday morning and uses the word "dopeish." Even then.

You'll learn to hate IKEA. Really. You'll shout about missing screws and cut yourself on folded sheets of plywood and swear to devote your life to finding and killing whoever came up with the illustrated instructions for assembling this piece of crap TV stand.

And then you'll learn to love this place.

I came here with your mother just after we found out she was pregnant. Fantasized about who you would be. (United beat City that day, I missed that game too.) And we came here with you in the stroller just after you were born. Fantasized about who you would grow up to be. And I allow myself to imagine once in a while that one day I might have the joy of walking around here, missing Manchester United games while we look at things for my grandchild. Because one day I'll look away for two seconds and when I turn around again you'll be all grown up.

And then I'll get my goddamn payback for all this.

Then I'll wake *you* up at half past five on a Sunday morning and throw up into *your* Xbox, let me tell you that right now. And then we'll come here and I'll give you good advice about life and everything and you'll roll your eyes and we'll have a huge fight over the best way to get those damn boxes into the back of the car. (You'll be wrong.)

Some of the very, very, very best days of our life will be in IKEA.

So play. Learn. Grow up. Follow your passions. Find someone to love. Do your best. Be kind when you can, tough when you need to be. Hold on to your friends. Don't go against the direction of the painted arrows in the floor. You'll be just fine.

But honestly, now. Tell me the truth. You've peed in the ball pool, haven't you? Great. Just great.

YES. I KNOW YOUR MOTHER SAID NO.

But seriously.

She thought "Santiago Bernabéu" was a red wine.

You can't listen to her.

RECIPE FOR FRIED SNICKERS ICE CREAM

(You'll thank me for this one day.)

You Need:

Flour
Water
Beer
Baking powder
A wok
Small pieces of bread
Enough oil that the City Health Department will announce you an enemy of the people
As many Snickers ice creams as you can carry
Someone else's kitchen

(If you use our kitchen and your mother finds out, you're also going to need a witness protection program.)

Do the Following:

Take the Snickers ice creams out of their wrappers and put on a plate in the freezer. Leave them there for 6 to 7 Football Manager games. They should be as stiff as a Keanu Reeves performance (other than the first *Matrix* film and parts of the third) when you take them out.

41

Mix equal parts flour and water and a tablespoon of baking powder. Heat the oil until it bubbles like the water in that cave where Flash Gordon goes to look for that girl.

Take out the Snickers ice creams. Dip in the flour/water goo. Drop into the oil. Leave to fry for 15 to 20 seconds until they start to look awesome. Take out. Eat immediately.

(I also put syrup, chocolate sauce, and Ben & Jerry's New York Super Fudge Chunk on mine. But if you feel like that's a bit unhealthy and want something fresher, you could definitely serve it with some kind of fruit instead. Banana, for example. In that case, you don't even have to change the oil. Just fry the banana in the same oil as the ice cream.)

This message will self-destruct in five seconds.

[BABY APPLAUDING IRONICALLY]

Yes. I've noticed that you've learned to clap.

And don't get me wrong, that's all lovely and good. Child psychologists say that hand clapping is closely linked to both coordination and creativity. A way for small children to express their identity. And that's just great and all that.

But, I mean. I just wish you would clap a bit more . . . enthusiastically. That's all. The way you do it now, it's really slow and quiet. It's almost like you're doing it . . . to prove a point. You know what I mean?

And yes, obviously I tried to use this to my advantage at first, like I guess all normal parents would. I started pretending I was constantly in a golf tournament and that you were the crowd just after I hit the fairway. I practiced my swing in the kitchen and gazed toward the horizon, and as I passed your walker I adjusted my cap in a concentrated manner and mumbled things like, "Mmm, now I just have to make it over the left bunker and then I can reach the green in two."

But now, I don't know how to explain it. Now you clap all demonstratively at moments when it's hard to interpret it as you being anything other than, well . . . sarcastic.

Like when I feed you. And I, to make the

whole thing more exciting, pretend that the spoon is an airplane. That's when you just give me a skeptical look once the spoon is in your mouth, and you swallow the food with the same expression your mother usually wears when I play air guitar. And then you clap.

Not for long. Not enthusiastically. Just three or four claps. Slow and quiet.

And it's really hard not to feel like you're saying, "There, clever idiot. You found my mouth. Shall we see if you can do it again?"

Honestly, it's really starting to affect my self-confidence.

I STILL DON'T GET IT.

Whenever your mother has given you breakfast, the kitchen looks like an advertisement for cleaning products. Whenever I give you breakfast, it looks like the part of *The Hunger Games* where everybody dies. There's something someone's not telling me here, dammit.

WHAT YOU NEED TO KNOW ABOUT SOCCER

I'm not saying you have to play soccer. Of course you don't. I'm not going to be one of those dads who puts pressure on you and stands on the sidelines screaming and shouting.

I'm just saying that things will be easier if you play soccer. That's all. You'll avoid having to take a lot of crap from your surroundings, that's all.

I mean, I can see you aren't all that interested right now. You actually seem to find dancing a lot more fun. And yes, we're not quite in agreement over whether I threw that ball *to* you or *at* you just now. But the minute your mother turns on music, you're suddenly bouncing through the living room like a jolly little Gummi Bear on prescription medication.

And it's not that there's anything WRONG with that. Not at all. Of course, you should dance if you want to.

I'm just saying that life as a little boy will be less complicated if you play soccer. That I'm worried about the alienation a different choice might cause. That's all.

And listen, you don't even need to PLAY soccer, all right? You just need to like watching it. It's just about being part of the group. Feeling accepted.

Not that there's anything *w-r-o-n-g* with doing other things, of course not. Like dancing or whatever. Or, you know, other things. Of course not. It's just that I want you to avoid that feeling of not fitting in. No one wants to feel like that. I know that sounds weird, but I just want you to know this is all about love.

It's important to feel a part of something. Not to feel like an outsider all the time.

Because, you know, I love soccer. Really, really love it. It's given me so much more than I could ever give back. And I want the same for you. I want you to experience everything soccer is and has been and can and should be, everything it could be for you and only you.

I want you to enjoy that magical life experience of finding your team. Because of loyalty, or as an act of rebellion. Because of geography, or history. To fit in. To stick out. Because of a defender with a cool name. Or just because of a pure, unexpected love.

Because that team just had the coolest-looking shirts.

And that shirt will follow you for a lifetime. Longer than most people. It'll become your superpower. You'll meet plenty of people who won't understand it, but regardless of where you end up in life, that shirt will give you ninety minutes of amnesia every week. And you'll discover that, sometimes, that's the most desired superpower of all.

Not that there's anything wrong with dancing. Not at all.

Or horse riding or synchronized swimming or anything like that, if you'd prefer that. Not at all. I'm not that kind of dad, you know? It's perfectly fine if you choose that instead.

Maybe you don't even want to do a sport. You might want to play golf instead! And that's all right *too*!

I don't have any prejudices.

It's just that I'm . . . you know. Worried about that feeling of being left out.

So I just want a chance to explain what soccer has given me.

Because it's not just about me taking you to a game and explaining the rules and strategies. Like how best to avoid the lines at the hot dog stands: you don't go there five minutes before halftime, you go five minutes before halftime is over, when all the other suckers are already heading back to their seats. (Or how you should always ask to have the fried onions in the bottom of the bun, as far away from the ketchup as possible, so you don't accidentally turn the entire seating section into a textured wallpaper when your team scores a goal. Experience.)

It's about other things too. Like how all the most magical fairy tales I can tell you about — how the smallest can become the greatest, even if just for a day — I've learned from soccer. Everything I know about second chances. About how there'll always be a new game. That every week ends with a Sunday. That we'll always get another opportunity to be perfect.

That, regardless of all other circumstances, it's always 0–0 to begin with.

When you grow up, people will often ask you about your first great love. And, for me, it was this. Maybe you won't like it at all. Maybe the idea of twenty-two millionaires with underarm tattoos and hair products you could make bulletproof vests out of running around on a lawn and throwing themselves to the ground like they've been shot with horse tranquilizers the second they find themselves in the same zipcode as a defensive goal line is just less appealing to you than to me.

I get that.

Fine.

You might end up hating soccer.

And I want you to know that I'll never, ever, ever love you any less in that case. Or be any less proud of you. You're my boy. When you were born, it was like someone carbonated the air in my lungs. Like you blew bubbles into my blood through a straw. My entire life was about nothing but me for twenty-five years, but then your mother came along and then you came along and now I wake up in the middle of the night several times a week and have to check you're both still breathing before I can get back to sleep. Can you grasp that? If I'd acted this way before I became someone's dad, they would have locked me up in a padded cell with an iPod full of dolphin songs.

I'm not afraid of saying I love you. It's just all the rest of it that scares the living crap out of me.

I'm afraid of what people will say if you don't play soccer. Afraid of the shame. The nicknames. The being left out. Afraid that they'll . . . you know.

I mean, maybe you'd rather take up sailing or ballet or pole vault or figure skating instead. And that's all right. I really want to be a father who says that and means it. It's okay! I want you to do whatever makes you happy, regardless of what anyone says.

I just want you to be prepared for the ignorance and the prejudices.

You don't *have* to like soccer. You can play chess. Or sing. Hell, if you decide to devote all your time to that thing they do in the Olympics where they run about on a mat in a gym hall accompanied by the *Titanic* soundtrack, waving two sticks with that kind of ribbon you use to wrap presents with at each end, I'll come to every bloody training session.

I'm just worried I won't understand it.

See, I don't want to be the dad all the other kids shake their heads at. The one who doesn't fit in among the rest of the parents. Someone you're ashamed of. The one who doesn't understand the thing you love. The one who disappoints you.

I know soccer. I don't know much about much else, but I know soccer. I barely know anything about art or fashion or literature or computers or building a roof or changing engine oil. I know very little about music.

I'm not always great at talking about feelings.

And I know all kids sooner or later reach a point in their lives where they realize their dads aren't actually superheroes. I'm not stupid. I just wish for it to take as long as possible. I wish we could at least have a couple of Sunday afternoons together, you and I. Something that's ours. Something I understand. Because I'm not afraid to say I love you, I'm just so deadly scared of all the rest.

Scared of the day when I lose my place in your life.

You don't have to like soccer.

I'm just trying to let you know that I'm really terrified of what things will be like if you don't. That feeling of being left out. The awkwardness. The loneliness.

Mine.

CHAOS THEORY

ME: You know that old saying "I feel less like his dad than I do like his parole officer"?

MY WIFE: That's not a saying.

ME: Well, it should be.

A-PAPA-CALYPSE NOW
Conversation with a good friend who has just finished his paternity leave

ME: So how was being home with the kids?

HIM: (*Scratching his beard nervously, glancing reflexively over his shoulder every now and then, mumbling absently*) Mmm. Definitely. Really good. Best thing I've done . . .

ME: Did you and the kids develop a bond like —

HIM: (*Pointing to my coffee cup in frustration*) What the hell, did you have to put that there?

ME: Huh?

HIM: (*Pointing furiously*) Do you have to put that cup there? It could tip over and BURN someone!

ME: (*Looking under the table*) Like who? There's no one down there . . .

HIM: (*Wide-eyed*) Not NOW, no! But it only takes a second! They come out of nowhere, the bastards!

(*Silence*)

HIM: (*Fingers drumming the table compulsively, staring up at the ceiling*) You're laughing, but just wait until you're there. Up to your neck in it. With no one to rely

57

on. You get paranoid, let me tell you. You think you know where they are, that you're in control, but they're silent. Like snakes . . .

(*Silence*)

MUTUAL FRIEND WHO DOESN'T HAVE KIDS: (*Glancing nervously at me*) When you said he was on "paternity leave," did you mean with kids or with the Vietcong?

WE ARE SEARCHING FOR THE ALLSPARK.

ME: What about this one? Where the hell's this one meant to go?

MY FRIEND J: Here, isn't it?

ME: Yeah. Must be. Put it there.

J: Doesn't fit.

ME: Put your weight into it!

J: I'm telling you it doesn't FIT!

ME: I don't understand how it can be this damn hard to put together a high chair.

J: It even says that it's "portable." What the hell do they mean by that?

ME: What about now? What about that?

J: I don't know . . . is that thing there really meant to stick out like that?

ME: No! But YOU fix it, then!

J: It feels like the whole thing is the wrong way round or something . . .

ME: These instructions are CRAP. Does it say anything useful on the box?

J: Yeah.

ME: What?

J: "Easy assembly."

(Silence. Both studying what really doesn't look like a correctly assembled high chair at all.)

J: We would've been terrible Transformers.

YOUR PARENTS' MARRIAGE: AN INTRODUCTION

Boy meets girl. Girl meets shoes. Shoes meet shoes. Boy empties basement. Shoes fill basement. Boy empties wardrobe. Shoes fill wardrobe. Girl goes into guest room and comes back out of walk-in closet. Boy and girl have baby. Girl meets baby shoes. Boy meets a more "practical" car. Girl meets shopping mall. Boy puts down foot. Girl is forbidden to buy new shoes before girl throws out old shoes.

Girl throws out boy's shoes.

YES. YES. CHILDHOOD TRAUMA THIS AND CHILDHOOD TRAUMA THAT.

I drew ONE small butcher's chart on the picture on the front of the packet of animal crackers. And suddenly, I'm referred to by my first, middle, and last names?

I think that's a bit much.

■ ■ ■ ■

What You Need to Know About Stuff

■ ■ ■ ■

All right, so someone scratched right down one side of our car with a key last night. But hey, it's fine.

I'm not angry at that someone for doing it.

Yes, it was completely unnecessary. It was. But that someone surely had their reasons. Someone might have had a bad day. Someone's girlfriend might have broken up with him. Someone might be a Tottenham fan. We shouldn't judge. We should have empathy.

And it's just a car, you know?

It's just a thing. It's just stuff.

And you should know that you'll collect a whole load of stuff during your lifetime, so you can't get too attached to any of it. It's not healthy. Because there'll be a lot of stuff. Long before you were born, an incredibly smart man called George Carlin taught your dad that. It's just as well you find out right away.

There'll be a LOT of stuff.

Small stuff. Big stuff. Bad stuff. Machine stuff whose only purpose is to produce more stuff. There's stuff that's meant to be part of the inside of other stuff. There's stuff that isn't even stuff, stuff you'll be holding at the checkout counter of the store while a nineteen-year-old who smells like hangover and cheese puffs gives you a condescending look and asks whether you have "the rest of the stuff you need to use this stuff?" And when you ask, "What stuff?" he'll shake his head so slowly that you'll think it's about to spin all the way around like an owl's and snort, "The accessory stuff! Without the accessory stuff, this is not even stuff! Without the accessory stuff, it's just a . . . thing!"

He'll say the word "thing" the way your grandma says very bad swear words. Like he's spitting it out. So you'll take it for granted that he knows about this stuff and ask to look at the accessory stuff, and then he'll sigh loudly and answer that you could have said that to begin with. Now he needs to go and check some stuff in the warehouse to see whether they have any of that stuff left. And by then you might start to feel that he's just making a thing out of this. But it's not your thing to point that out.

Because people like stuff. New stuff. Even newer stuff. Stuff to replace old stuff with and old stuff that is so old it becomes retro stuff and starts being used instead of new stuff. Let me tell you: it's fun stuff.

Sometimes we have to get rid of stuff to make room for new stuff, and then we start to miss the old stuff so much that we have to build new stuff that pretends to be the old stuff.

Like when we put TV screens on the treadmills at the gym and then play videos of trees on them, so that we feel like we're running through the forest. Yes, I know what you're thinking: "Why don't you just go running in the forest to begin with?" And it's completely okay to wonder that. You don't know any better. But, you see, we had to cut down the trees in the forest in order to build a highway so we could drive our cars to the gym. And yes, I can already see what you're thinking: "Why did you have to cut down the trees?" But hey, what did you want us to do? They were standing in the middle of the highway!

It's complicated stuff to explain.

So let me just make it really clear that I'm not angry at this someone for scratching the car. The car's just stuff.

And we can never allow stuff to become more important than people. Like you. I mean, I've thrown away all my best stuff to make room for your stuff. Because your stuff is more important. And my God, you have a lot of stuff. All parents with small children love to complain about your stuff. "These kids sure have a lot of STUFF!" we say as soon as we see one another. As though it's your fault. As though you're the ones buying it all. As though you're the ones at the store staring at lumps of black rubber or whatever with some stupid ghost painted on it that cost sixty dollars, thinking, "Am I a bad father if I don't buy this crap?"

And then the guy at the store grins and thumps you on the back and says, "You really can't put a price on a child's *safety*, can you?" And you don't grin back because it's all too clear that actually you can: sixty dollars. It says so right there. And then you buy the crap. Telling yourself this is what parenting is.

And if you only knew how much crap for children there is out there. The worst crap is actually the crap we bought before you were even born. Like a toy sheep containing a speaker that was meant to simulate "whale song" and help you sleep better. Why wasn't that crap shaped like a whale? Huh? That still bothers me.

Crap. Everywhere, crap. The overwhelming majority isn't even good crap. It's just crappy crap. And as soon as you have a child, you need crap for everything. You need special crap just to become compatible with the crap you already own. Crap for the car. Crap for the kitchen table. Crap for the bathroom. Don't even get me started about the amount of crap you need for poop. I came home from the store right after you were born and your mother shouted "Did you buy diapers?" and I was all "Of course I bought diapers!" and she took them out of the bag and looked deeply skeptical and read the packaging and was all "You bought diapers for babies aged six to nine months?" and I was all "Yeah, but that's just a recommendation, really" and she was all "He's nine days old!" and I was all "Don't you think I know that?!" and she was all "Apparently not!!!" and then she looked into the bag again and said "These wet wipes are perfumed" and I was all "No" and she was all "Yes" and I was all "No" and she was all "It says 'perfumed' on them" and I was all "That's what they want you to think, yes!" and she looked in the bag again and said "What's this?" and I was all "I think it's a rain cover for a charcoal barbecue grill" and she said "Why the hell did you buy a rain cover for a —" and I was all "BECAUSE I PANICKED!!! ALL RIGHT???" and then she said "Okaaay . . ." and rolled her eyes and I was all "You go ahead and roll your eyes! But you don't know what it's like out there! There are five hundred goddamn different sorts of diapers! The baby section is as big as an airplane hangar. I tried to find the kind you wanted but there were so many! So, so, so many diapers! Perfumed, unperfumed, with Winnie-the-Pooh on them, without Winnie-the-Pooh, with Velcro fastenings, with elastic, like pants, not like pants, some hypoallergenic ones, some that come with a free computer game, some that give you frequent flyer miles, like . . . WHAT THE HELL!?" and she said "Just calm down, Fredrik" and I was all "YOU calm down!" and she was all "Why are you getting so angry?" and I was all "Because a load of other fathers appeared! And they were all bam-bam-bam, knew exactly which ones they needed. Boom-boom, straight in the basket! And I was standing there like some clown, feeling like everyone was staring at me, until eventually I just GRABBED SOMETHING!"

Your mother doesn't understand what it

was like. She sat here at home like some kind of bureaucrat, giving out orders. But out there in the field, the shit was real! In the jungle, you only have a few seconds to make the right decision!

And . . . crap. You end up drowning in crap. You think you're going to be the cool young dad who just chills and never loses his temper, but then one day you're standing in front of the baby food shelf and realize that there are, like, seven different types of milk substitute and then you just lie down on the floor and cry.

So. You know.

I'm not angry about the scratch on the car. I'm not angry that I had to call the insurance company. I'm not angry that we'll have to do without our own car for over a week while it's repainted.

It's just that half of all the crap you need once you have a child isn't even ready-to-use crap. It's the kind of crap you have to assemble. It needs screwing and fastening and applying until your hallway looks like MacGyver has been smoking Black Afghan in the bathtub at the house of an old woman who never throws away newspapers.

All my weekends now look like an episode of *Handy Manny* that Disney decided to cancel because Manny went crazy and started screaming swear words and threatening to "punch the mother#%&^er who wrote these b#%&€#%t instructions in the f#!&#%g face!"

So I'm not angry at that someone because that someone scratched the car. Not at all.

Not angry that someone took what the insurance man referred to as a "probable key-like object" and dragged it along the whole rear of the car, the entire back door, and a bit of the front one.

Not angry about all the paperwork.

Not angry about the whole thing itself.

There's just one tiny, tiny, tiny detail I still want this someone to know.

And it's that I had to spend an HOUR today refitting your baby car seat AGAIN just because we were going to be using the rental car. I'll track someone down for that.

And I'll kill someone.

But, I mean. You know. Other than that: I'm not angry.

It's just that before you become a parent yourself, you think all parents are superheroes. You think that everything about having kids seems incredibly messy and hard, but you're counting on nature just solving it for you somehow. You'll get bitten by a radioactive midwife or be in a mysterious "accident" and wake up in a secret military hospital with a steel skeleton or something like that. It'll sort itself out.

But that's not what happens. The only superpower I've seen so far was when your mother developed an incredible sense of smell during pregnancy. And I'll be completely honest with you, that was the most useless superpower ever. I wasn't allowed to cook bacon at home for almost a year.

So it's without superpowers that you come home from the hospital with your newborn child and feel utterly abandoned and terrified. You look at the hospital staff as they discharge you from the maternity ward like they're leaving you to die in the desert. Like they're refusing to open the door to that village of survivors at the end of *I Am Legend* and just letting the zombies catch up to you.

You get home and you sit and watch your child sleep and wonder exactly who's meant to take responsibility for this now. Because it can't possibly be us. I drink juice straight from the carton and your mother never puts the DVDs back in the case. We're not cut out for this kind of thing. Someone should have done some kind of test. Put their foot down. When Sims 2 came out, I stopped playing because I felt like it was too much responsibility. I'm pretty sure that's not being "parent material."

So what do you do?

You panic. And you buy stuff. That's what you do.

Ergonomic and organic and pedagogic and anatomically correct stuff. You hear people say, "You *have* to have one of these!" And you immediately think, "Yeah, maybe we do, that does actually sound sensible." Cuddly animals and laser thermometers and teething rings and a potty that looks like Jabba the Hutt and a plastic tortoise that plays Mozart when you poke it in the crotch with a stick. It's like when you watch the shopping channel drunk and realize that your life won't be complete until you own a tool for cutting onions into stars. Or when you go to Thailand for two weeks and decide that dreadlocks make you look great.

So, you buy all that crap. And then you buy even more crap, telephone crap and video camera crap and computer crap, just so you can document yourselves using all the original crap. As though your children were some kind of scientific experiment. I'm not exaggerating when I say that nothing has revolutionized the way my generation interacts with yours more than when the iPhone 4 came out with the camera on the front, so we could actually sit next to one another while I watched you on the display.

There was a time before selfies, you know. And it was HORRIBLE.

This is my life now.

I've become one of those parents who decides that their kid is a genius because he worked out how to turn up the volume on the stereo. You pay seven hundred dollars for an iPad and then call up Mensa because your child manages to work out how to unlock the keypad by the time he's one and a half. And the woman on the other end doesn't say it straight to your face. But you can, so to speak, tell from her dogged breathing that she wants to shout "It's a KEYPAD LOCK! It's hardly the genetic code for a cure for prostate cancer, it's a frikkin' *k-e-y-p-a-d l-o-c-k.* Have you ever thought that maybe your kid is not a genius, but it might just be you who's a bit of an IDIOT?!"

She doesn't just come out and say it. She doesn't. But you can tell that's what she's thinking.

It's in moments like those that I realize we might have given you too much stuff. We might have given you the wrong crap. I might have given you the wrong values. Been a bad role model.

Because, Christ. I'm not going to *kill* that someone who scratched the car. I'm not crazy. It's just a thing you say.

It's just a car, you know?

I'll settle this conflict rationally. Track down that someone and have a grown-up conversation with them. Voice my disapproval with this someone's behavior. At the very most, I might break into someone's apartment when someone isn't home and do unmentionable things to all of someone's karate trophies.

Like an adult. Because it's just . . . you know. Stuff. It doesn't matter. But at the same time . . . now that we're actually talking about it . . .

I'm just realizing while I'm writing this that when I go to pick up the repainted car in a week's time, I'll have to give back the rental car.

And then I'll have to fit that damn car seat into ours again. Give me a second.

Yeah. All right. I'm probably going to kill someone.

FIRST DAY OF PRESCHOOL

I'm not saying I'm picking favorites here. Absolutely not.

And I don't want to put any pressure on you whatsoever when it comes to which of the other kids in your preschool I think you should be friends with.

All I'm saying is that at the information meeting, the teachers explained that during the first days of settling in, they would ask us parents to go and wait in another room.

And there was one parent who immediately asked, "Which room?" And then spent the rest of the guided tour of the building walking around that room with an iPhone in the air, checking where the best 4G coverage was.

I'm not putting ANY pressure on you or anything like that. But I think that parent and I would get on well. That's all I'm saying.

You're Not Saying Anything. But It Feels Like This Is What You're Saying.

All right. So you're, like, twelve weeks old.

And I get up in the morning. Just after five. Pick you up. Go out into the hallway. Stub my toe on the doorframe. Hit my head on a light. Go into the bathroom. Bash my knee on the door. Put you down on the changing table. Knock over a pile of washcloths. Try to keep one hand on you on the changing table as I bend down to pick up the washcloths. Manage to poke you in the eye. You get angry. I hit my head on the underside of the changing table, reach around to turn on the tap, knock two perfume bottles into the sink. One of them breaks. Knock your trousers onto the floor. Attempt to keep one hand on you while I try to wet one of the washcloths without cutting myself on the glass, all while I try to avoid knocking over the rest of the contents of the bathroom cabinet and attempt to pick up your trousers from the floor with my toes like a monkey. When I eventually manage that and you're wearing your trousers again, I realize I haven't put a diaper on you. I pull off your trousers, put on a diaper, manage to knock over a huge basket of shampoo bottles or whatever the hell they are. Try to pick up the smaller bottles one by one with my toes. Manage to stick my finger in your nose. You get angry again.

And once I'm finished, have turned off the water, gathered up all the little pieces of glass and the bottles of whatever it is, picked you up, and carried you back through the apartment to your bed, I realize I've put your diaper on the wrong way. And that you are, once again, not wearing any trousers.

And you lie there so still, just looking at me so thoughtfully. Our eyes meet.

And you know how some parents seem to know exactly what their child's first words will be?

That's when I start to get an uneasy feeling that yours will be: "You are the weakest link. Good-bye."

THE ART OF PREDICTING IF A PRACTICAL JOKE IS APPROPRIATE

Let's suppose that you and I meet a friend of mine, who has a daughter around your age, in the local supermarket. My friend's girlfriend is busy ordering something over at the fish counter, so my friend and I immediately come up with the incredibly funny idea of swapping you kids in the strollers while she's not looking, just to see how long it takes her to realize when she comes back that this is not actually her kid. Funny, huh?

Yeah. So let's suppose I then get maybe a bit overenthusiastic about the whole thing and sort of run away through the store with their daughter in my stroller, to hide.

And then suppose I, let's say, have maybe never actually *met* my friend's girlfriend before. And then let's suppose that the first thing she sees when she turns around from the fish counter five seconds later isn't her boyfriend standing next to you, giggling, like he and I both planned. No, let's suppose instead that the first thing she sees is a fairly chubby guy with a baseball hat who she's never seen before in her life, running down the dairy aisle with her one-year-old daughter.

Then it's quite possible that this whole

idea was a LITTLE bit funnier in theory than it was in practice. Let's suppose that.

So . . .

When your mother's and my friends come over to tell us that half of the couple is pregnant, apparently it's okay for me to share in their general joy at the news. It's also completely fine for me to high-five the nonpregnant half of the couple and to offer him a drink. It's even considered, under certain circumstances, perfectly socially acceptable to punch him on the shoulder and grunt things like "You old dog."

It's also okay, to a limited extent, to talk about how tired women get during the first few months of pregnancy and even make jokes about how your mother did virtually nothing but sleep during the first twelve weeks.

It's actually even okay to go so far as to happily exclaim, "I've *never* played as many video games as I did those weeks!"

This is all okay. What is not okay, on the other hand, is to refer to those weeks as "the best of the entire pregnancy." It's very important, that last part. Crucial.

MARKED FOR LIFE

Apparently, lots of fathers get tattoos to celebrate their newborn children. Portraits. Dates of their births. Those kinds of things. And I've thought about it too. But in that case, I want it to be something really symbolic. Something that will really sum up the relationship you and I have, you know, as father and son? Right now, I'm thinking about a tiny, tiny tribal tattoo in the form of a puddle of milk puke on my shoulder.

■ ■ ■ ■

What You Need to Know About Being a Man

■ ■ ■ ■

They say that it's a father's job to teach his son what it means to be a man. But I don't know. They say that sooner or later the majority of men turn into their fathers. But I hope that isn't true.

Your grandfathers are different kinds of men than I am. Prouder and tougher men. With different kinds of skills. For example, they know exactly how to determine the quality of cars just by kicking the tires. And if you give them any electronic product, any one at all, they can judge whether you've paid too much for it in three seconds just by weighing it in their hands. (You have always paid too much for it.)

They haven't been wrong in a discussion since the midseventies. (And even then, they weren't *wrong,* they just admitted that someone else might also be a *little* bit right.)

They don't stop for directions. They don't ask for help. They never argue about money,

only about principles. They'll never understand why you would pay anyone to do
something you could just as easily do
yourself (and their sons will never understand why you would want to do anything
all wrong by yourself instead of hiring an
expert to begin with, which is actually the
cause of almost all of our intergenerational
conflicts). They're a different breed, pure
and simple. They know how an extension
cord works. You can wake them up in the
middle of the night and they'll tell you
today's mortgage interest rate down to the
decimal point. No matter what you buy,
they'll look at you with disappointment in
their eyes and ask you what it cost. And
though you'll lie and lower the price by 20
percent, they'll still say, "$29.95?! They
TRICKED you! I know a place where you
could've gotten it for . . ."

Every time you go over to their houses,
they'll force you to tell them the exact route
you took to get there. And when you finally
admit that you didn't take their "special
shortcut" this time either, since you don't
feel all that confident driving over train
tracks and are actually pretty sure there are
bats in those caves, they'll look at you the
way William Wallace looks at the traitor at
the end of *Braveheart*.

That's the kind of men they are.

They can go out onto a lawn at dawn, empty-handed, and come back in from a newly built deck. I mean, come on. The only thing I've ever finished with my own two hands is Grand Theft Auto IV. (And I cheated.)

Your grandfathers built their own houses before Google even existed. Can you comprehend the scope of that accomplishment? They're not people. They're Swiss Army knives with beards. They're proud and they're tough and it's entirely possible that they don't always say the right thing at the right moment. This whole idea of shared parental leave wasn't exactly on the agenda when they became fathers, and it's entirely possible that they might not always be great at talking about things you can't kick the tires of or weigh in your hand. But they're hard workers. They've pulled their weight in society. They can file their own taxes and fix a microwave oven and put up a tent and change the oil in a Ford Escort. These men tamed nature. They survived the beginning of time. In the total wilderness. They didn't even have Wi-Fi when they grew up. Just think about that. Their entire childhood was an episode of *Survivor*.

Seriously.

You know that technique of opening a beer bottle with another beer bottle? It took me, no kidding, well into my twenties to realize that my dad hadn't invented that. The first time I saw someone else do it, my first thought wasn't "Wow, I guess Dad didn't come up with that after all." My first thought was: "WOW! It's spreading!"

I don't know whether that says more about my dad or me.

But at some point, I stopped giving him credit for things. Somewhere along the way, my generation started to take his generation for granted. And now here we are, with our specialist skills and our CrossFit and our designer-cut beards and our Facebook statuses, but we don't know how to fix a leaking faucet. Or what a camshaft is. Or how to build a deck.

We kind of messed up, to be honest. The whole point of evolution should be to make each generation smarter, stronger, and quicker than the one before. And sure, my generation is great at a lot of things. Modern things. No thirty-year-old is ever going to be beaten by a sixty-year-old in a game of Super Mario Kart, you can bet your behind on that.

But if the apocalypse comes, if the world

is devastated by a World War III fought with nuclear weapons, and what's eventually left of humanity peers up out of its bunker a few years later to see a barren, unforgiving, desolate landscape, and these last few survivors decide to gather the very smartest, toughest, and most capable individuals who are left to lead the rebuilding of our species: well, no one's going to come looking for my generation.

Or, no, that's unfair. Of course they'll come looking for us.

To ask where our parents are.

Not because my generation's skills will be useless in that situation, that's not what I'm saying at all. We're just not going to be able to use a single one of them until someone has reinvented electricity.

So I want you to know that it's not easy to teach you what a man is. I'll do what I can. I'll try to explain this miraculous place of advanced technological discoveries and worldwide information networks and democratic revolutions and medical advances. But I'll never be able to teach you half as much as the men who can tell you how we got here.

You take their feelings for granted, I know that. You don't find it strange at all that they whisper "I love you" in your ear all the time.

But you taught them those words. They became different men when you came along.

Because it's quite possible that the men from your grandfathers' generation made a mistake or two in their own parenting when my generation was young. But if that's the case, they're making up for it now by covering over the cracks and faults in ours.

So it's not easy to teach you what a man is. Masculinity changes. That's the whole idea.

It's almost impossible even to discuss it with other adults. For a society that constantly claims we shouldn't make any distinctions between men and women, we sure spend an awful lot of time defining exactly what those differences are. The discussion can get confusing. And by that, I don't mean "confusing" in the same way as when they've moved everything around in our local 7-Eleven (again). I mean confusing in the sense of that polar bear turning up in the first season of *Lost,* and we were all "What the HELL? Is that a POLAR BEAR?" (You haven't seen *Lost.* I know. But let's just say it was . . . weird.)

I know I'm still learning about what the word "inequality" really means. Every day. I have to. I'm a white, heterosexual, Western European man with an education and a job.

There's not a single organism in the entire universe who knows *less* about inequality than me.

But I'm trying to learn. And I hope you'll know more than I did.

That you'll never fear justice. Never misinterpret the fight for equality as a war between the sexes. That you'll never believe that a woman doesn't deserve the same rights or freedoms or chances that you do. I hope you'll know that, above all, most people are not looking for special treatment, most people don't want everything to be the same for everyone, most people just want things to be FAIR for everyone. I hope you'll get that, way faster than I did. And I hope that you'll never get it into your head that just because a woman deserves every opportunity you do, you have to stop holding the door open for her when you can. That you'll never think it's impossible to be equals and behave like a gentleman at the same time. Because, as your grandmothers will teach you, that's rubbish. There is plenty that can be said about your grandfathers' generation of men, but they wouldn't have had time to learn about everything in the world if the women of their generation hadn't taken care of everything else while they did.

And I've done what I can to teach you to never feel threatened by strong women. I married the strongest one I've ever met.

The world will constantly try to tell you that it's possible to divide every single human quality or skill or characteristic into those that are "male" and those that are "female." But I don't know. I might win a fight against your mother. It wouldn't exactly be "gorilla vs. bear," you know? More "gorilla vs. koala."

But she would destroy me in a footrace, no matter the distance. And she's way funnier than I am. And she gets people. She's someone everyone trusts. I can easily think of a hundred people who would follow her blindly into war. I can barely get people to follow me on Twitter.

In terms of brains, though, it's harder to measure for sure. I mean, on the one hand she's definitely smarter than I am, everyone knows that. But on the other hand: I got her to marry me. So I still feel like I have one up on her.

And I've noticed that you've already learned that your ability to make her laugh largely determines your chances of being able to get away with stuff you've messed up. Hold on to that skill. It'll take you a long way. It's what brought me this far.

And when she laughs. My God. I never feel like more of a man than I do right then.

So . . . it's not easy to teach you what a man is. It's different things for different people. With different people.

People used to shout, "Stand up like a real man," in every possible context when I was a teenager. It took me a good few years into my twenties to realize that real men can also stay seated, shut up, and listen. And admit when they're wrong. So don't make the same mistakes I did. Never go to a game of anything and shout, "You're playing like a woman!" at an athlete, as though that word were the definition of weakness. One day, you'll be holding a woman's hand as she gives birth and then that'll make you feel more ashamed than you've ever felt about anything. Words matter. Be better.

And never let the terms of masculinity be dictated by someone who thinks it's bound up with sexuality. If you really want to know something about what it means to be a man, just ask Gareth Thomas, who stood up in a locker room and told his teammates on the Welsh national rugby team that he was gay. I might not know much about much in this world, but I know for damn sure that no one in that locker room was more of a man at that moment than he was.

I want you to always remember that you can become whatever you want to become, but that's nowhere near as important as knowing that you can be exactly who you are. I hope I was just the dysfunctional prototype. I hope you tell me a million times over what an idiot I am.

Because I can't teach you how to be a man. That's something you need to teach me. That's the only way forward.

Because they say that, sooner or later, all men turn into their fathers. And I really hope that's not the case.

I hope you become much better.

That you never stop running toward the gate, laughing, when one of your grand-fathers picks you up from preschool. That you never stop making them laugh so much the walls shake. Because the only thing you can give to men who already have everything is a second chance. And you're all of their second chances. Every day.

They're tough and they're proud. They make mistakes and they have faults. But all the best things I know about being a man are things I've learned from them. And they became different men when you arrived.

Better men.

We all did.

WE INTERRUPT THIS BROADCAST TO SEND A SHORT MESSAGE TO YOUR MOTHER.

Yes, it's possible that I should have paid more attention to the fact that we've started giving the baby real food now. And yes, I can agree that maybe I didn't listen as closely as I should have when you explained the exact circumstances around that.

But I don't care what you say. Because if I see ten small plastic Tupperware containers of homemade mashed potatoes in the fridge, I'm going to eat those mashed potatoes. Because it's my duty. Because evolution demands it. And, most of all, because I love mashed potatoes.

How was I meant to know they were for the BABY? A few months ago, we counted takeaway pizza as "basically homemade supper," and now you're standing here, making your own baby food? Who are you? Mary Poppins?

Stop giving me the silent treatment and open the door! It's really cold out here!

The Art of Not Letting Your Pride Get in the Way of a Good Result

During the time your mother was pregnant and was not supposed to climb ladders

GOOD FRIEND: I see Fredrik fixed the light in the bathroom!

YOUR MOTHER: Yeah . . . actually, it wasn't Fredrik. It was my dad.

GOOD FRIEND: Oh. Right.

ME: Stop looking like that. I . . . you know . . . I had a lot of other things to do!

GOOD FRIEND: (*Clearing throat*) Of course. Of course. I actually think it's quite big of you to let your father-in-law come over and fix things.

(*Awkward silence*)

ME: What do you mean by that?

GOOD FRIEND: No, it's just, you know . . . most men probably wouldn't be able to admit that they can't fix a light by themselves, you know? They probably wouldn't be able to swallow their pride and call their father-in-law for help. Most men probably would've seen that as a threat to their masculinity . . .

ME: What's THAT supposed to mean?

GOOD FRIEND: I'm just saying.

YOUR MOTHER: Actually, you'd be surprised by how *few* things threaten Fredrik's masculinity after he's been going to the toilet in the dark for three days.

IT'LL BE WRONG NO MATTER WHAT YOU DO. THAT'S HOW IT FEELS.

You know when I've just wheeled the stroller into the elevator and realize I've forgotten something in the apartment? And then I quickly run back in to grab it. And while I'm in there, I think: "Crap, hang on a second, did I have time to press the button?" And right then, I hear the lift doors close in the stairwell. And I realize that, damn it, you and the stroller just went downstairs on your own.

So I run down the stairs, panicking slightly but also thinking that "Ah, it'll be fine, I must be quicker than the elevator." But just as I make it down, one of the neighbors presses the button on their floor. So the doors close right before my eyes, and the elevator goes upward again.

And I'm left standing there.

And I realize that I now have two choices: I can either run up the stairs. And risk being the father who manages not just to leave his child alone in the elevator, but who also doesn't manage to make it upstairs before the neighbors step into the elevator and come down to the ground floor, realize there's no one there, and call social services.

Or else I can stay here and wait. And be the father who not only leaves his child

100

alone in the elevator, but also then stands around nonchalantly thinking, "Uff, he'll probably be back . . ."

You know when that happens?

Could you try not to look quite so smug when the neighbors find you?

WHAT YOU NEED TO KNOW ABOUT KNOW ABOUT GOD AND AIRPORTS

So. This is an airport. This is where the planes live. And this is the conveyor belt for the luggage. Pretty cool, huh? I know. We use this so we don't have to go and get our bags from the plane ourselves. We just chill right here, and the bags come to us. Like we're Harry Potter.

And sure, I know you might be wondering why we're here and why I'm telling you this.

(But seriously, the bags come *to* us! It's like a bag treadmill. Back when I was a child, that sort of technology was considered so mind-blowing it was the highlight of the whole frikkin' family vacation, but you just go ahead and roll your eyes at your father now, that's just fine — we didn't have iPads and crap like that back then, so sure, don't let me bore you with any other REVOLUTIONARY ADVANCES for the whole of HUMANITY!)

But . . . here's what I'm thinking: I am

your father, after all. And I reckon the whole point of fatherhood is to explain to you how the world works. Right? Right. And I'm thinking that one of those typical questions all children wonder about sooner or later is: "Why are there wars?" Right? Right. All kids want peace on Earth. Most adults do too, I suppose. That's where this gets complicated.

And I'm thinking that if you ask "Why are there wars?" of ten randomly chosen people, at least half of them will say something like "Well, y'know, all wars are basically about reliiigion. Like, everyone knows that!"

So I'm thinking, as we're standing here talking about wars, that maybe I should tell you a little something about God too.

And yes, I realize you might think that the luggage conveyor belt in the airport is a strange place for a conversation about God. But I want you to pay attention to the yellow line in the floor. The one where it says PLEASE STAND BEHIND THE YELLOW LINE. I genuinely never feel more spiritual than when I see that line.

So: I will never tell you whether you should be religious or not. Or even if you should believe in God. That's a thing between God and you, or not. As long as you are kind to your mother and don't murder or steal or start supporting Manchester City or any other horrible thing like that, I genuinely don't care whether your moral compass is shaped by an old book or a box of jam doughnuts. But if I'm going to try to explain to you how I feel the world works here, it would be more than a bit odd to leave out the topic of religion.

See, God is incredibly important to people. Particularly to the people who don't actually believe in God. In my experience, no one wants to talk to you as much about God as the people who claim they absolutely DO NOT want to talk to you about God. And sooner or later, one of them will stare at you and ask, "But if God EXISTS, then why are there WARS?" If you study religion or philosophy at a university, this is called the "Theodicy Problem" or the "Problem of Evil," but if you're in a bar, it will probably be called the "got-you-there-am-I-right-or-am-I-right-huh?" argument.

I've been thinking about this a lot. Like . . . a lot. So much so that I spent four years and a small fortune in student loans at a pretty decent university studying religion and philosophy trying to find an answer to it. And here's what I came back with:

God created people. All right? Even if you don't believe in God, just assume that God created people. All right. And then the people created a bunch of stuff. Mostly the stuff was crap. And God was all like "Wait, what are you doing with all that crap?" and the people immediately got all defensive like "What? Nothing! It's our stuff! Why do you care?" and God was trying to be diplomatic and pointed and said "All right, but . . . where are you going with that thing? It doesn't look safe" and the people rolled their eyes and said "We're going OUT! Who are you? The cops?" and God was all "I'm sorry, I didn't mean to . . . but are you really . . . that doesn't look like such a good idea" and the people were all "Stop being so overprotective, we're not CHILDREN! You created us, like, FIFTEEN minutes ago!" and God was all "Fine, fine, all right, all right." And then the people took all their stuff, mostly crap, out into the world. And the world . . . well . . . a lot of bad stuff happened to it, to be honest. And then God mumbled "Told you" but did the people then stop and say "Ooops, our bad"? No. The people immediately turned to God and looked incredibly upset and cried "Why didn't you stop us! You could've stopped us? Now this is YOUR fault!"

Get it? Because that's our nature, us humans.

God, if you believe in God, was still pretty cool, you know? Dug out irrigation ditches and created gardens and came up with a way of keeping steaks and pork chops fresh longer by giving them legs and calling them "animals." (Best. Idea. Ever.) And then God turned on all the lights and said "Here's light, here's a world, just for you!" And the people yawned nonchalantly, wriggled into swimsuits and got themselves tribal tattoos, and toddled off to check things out. And at first, maybe things went pretty well. But after a while, the people discovered that God, like most contractors, hadn't made everything EXACTLY the way the people wanted everything. Because people like everything a CERTAIN way and "God, like, never listens, 'cause, for example, like, I've never liked the color 'sky blue' and now the whole sky is, like, sky blue and how am I supposed to, like . . . live with that? Huh?" And then, of course, the people just assumed they could have done all this world-creating stuff much better themselves. And so they started to tinker with God's creation.

And God looked at them, mumbling "Please don't pull that . . . it's not supposed to . . ." but the people just said "Talk to the hand!" and did a really annoying thing with their hands. And at that point, God just massaged God's temples and took a really, really, really long walk.

While God was gone, people decided they wanted more stuff. Sure, they already had loads of stuff, but you know, by then all that stuff had turned to crap. So the people decided to get rid of all that. At first, it was a painfully slow process, but then a woman (or a man, it could have been a man) of the people discovered fire. And that worked awesomely, of course. Fire became the hottest thing around. It actually got so popular that the people, once they'd set fire to all of their own crap, decided to take fire out on tour to set fire to other people's crap too. It got rave reviews. Several people called fire "the best thing to come out of banging two rocks together since gravel!" But since the fire was a bit tricky to move around, people had to come up with a better method of transport. So a woman (or a man! Let's not just assume it was a woman, once in a while men find things out on their own too!) of the people invented the wheel.

Immediately, though, the rest of the people were of course really skeptical, and started asking "Sure, so you've invented the wheel, have you? But how are you going to structure a business model around it? Is it scalable? Could it be a franchise? What's your plan here?" But then another person turned up, with a beard and a turtleneck (the shirt, not just that piece of the turtle, which would have been weird, because this is by all accounts an unweird story), painted the wheel white, and started to sell it for double the price to art directors in Stockholm. And everyone screamed "GENIUS!" to the turtleneck. And the guy who invented the wheel muttered "Never mind" and went back to his garage.

And so the years passed, and one day a couple of women (or men) were out in the desert, with their wheel and their fire, burying a dead body (because remember, a good friend helps you move, but a great friend helps you move a dead body), and they dug a little too deep, and suddenly the ground began to pee all over them. They had discovered oil.

And that was obviously great. They ran back to the rest of the people and they high-fived one another and someone came running with their fire and was all "Wait! What happens if we combine it with this?" And so they did. And then someone else said "But what happens if we combine it with the wheel?" And so they did that too. And then they looked at it and were all like "Well, what is it?" And then the turtleneck showed up, painted it white, and just started making up words like "combustion" and "engine" and everyone screamed "GENIUS!" And off they went.

This was obviously a phenomenal breakthrough for the whole of humanity. Now people could drive around setting fire to one another's crap all day, plus they could do it in a line! They had invented rush-hour traffic. (And, completely by chance, they had also discovered the comical concept of "irony" by naming something standing completely frikkin' still after something moving incredibly fast.)

And the people loved their rush-hour traffic. Oh, how they loved it. They loved it so much that they built small metal boxes to place on top of their wheels and their engines so that they could stay in there all winter. They cut small round holes inside the metal boxes and invented small paper containers that fit perfectly in the holes, and into these containers they poured a black liquid they'd also invented, which had the sole function of making you not need to sleep once you drank it. And that meant they could stay up in the rush-hour traffic all night. Hurrah!

For a few years, of course, this was paradise. People carpe'd the diem like they had never carpe'd it before, let me tell you. Until one of them became a little bit too ambitious and discovered that you could pour foamed milk into the black liquid and call it a "latte," which obviously made everyone incredibly stressed and agitated, because it was completely impossible to get the cows to sit still inside the metal boxes in rush-hour traffic. And then a few of the people thought "There MUST be a better way to travel than this!"

And so they invented the airplane.

And just then, God came back from his walk. And God looked down at the people and, in all his goodness and Godliness, descended to Earth, where he kneeled down and painted a yellow line a few feet from the luggage conveyor belt. And God said "If everyone stands behind this yellow line, then EVERYONE will be able to see their bags coming."

But then one of the people (I'm not saying it was a man, it could have been a woman, but let's be honest, it was Robert from down the street) looked at the yellow line and was all "Nooo! I want to stand cloooooser!" And so Robert crossed the line. And then the rest of the people also crossed the line. And now no one can see their bags coming.

And that's why we have wars.

Because people are really bloody stupid.

So I don't care whether you're religious or not. I just want you and me to at least agree over the fact that if you can't put ten people in a room and tell them, "If you cross the yellow line, it will benefit you just a little but ruin things completely for everyone else, but if you stay behind the yellow li— DAMN IT, ROBERT!" well, we've probably passed the point where all this stopped being God's responsibility. Agreed?

I know that in a year or two, you'll learn how to talk, and after that you'll pretty quickly enter that phase where, regardless of what I say, you'll always ask "Why?" Well, I can help you out right now by telling you that in 95 percent of the cases, the answer to "Why?" will be "Because people are really bloody stupid."

All right? All right.

So when your mother gets here in a couple of minutes and wonders why we missed our bags twice while they were passing, that's what we'll say. We won't tell her it was because we were playing Minecraft on my phone and lost focus. Agreed? Agreed.

THIS IS NOT GOING WELL. I'M AWARE.

I'm sure the other dads probably have some kind of neat, pedagogical explanation for this.

Something about the birds and the bees and the stork making a delivery and all that.

But, well, you know. I got tangled up in my own explanation here. I became overly ambitious. I wanted to build a realistic story.

I should have kept it simple.

I know.

But I started the story with "so your dad" and continued it with "or wait, let's start here instead, you see the *storks* will . . ." and . . . here we are. If you go racing off to preschool now and tell the other kids that your dad did those things to a stork, there's a real risk that Dad will get arrested. All right?

We need to start over. And just to avoid misunderstandings, I'll just say it like it is. Okay?

Okay.

I had sex with your mother.

You're gonna need a few years to process this.

I'm sorry. I really should have just told you about storks.

I THINK OF YOU A BIT LIKE I THINK OF THE T. REX IN *JURASSIC PARK*.
At five thirty in the morning, when you're staring at me, I know only one thing.

The tiniest. Little. Movement.

And it's all over.

THIS PARENTHOOD THING DIDN'T COME WITH INSTRUCTIONS, THAT'S ALL I'M SAYING.

You spit on the napkin.

Then you wipe the child's face with the napkin. You don't spit straight onto the child.

My bad.

■ ■ ■ ■

WHAT YOU NEED TO KNOW ABOUT WHAT HAPPENED TO THE SINGING PLASTIC GIRAFFE

■ ■ ■ ■

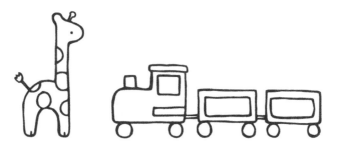

Well, it means nothing to you now, of course.

But I want you to know that the stuff people remember from their childhood, they really are the strangest of things.

Like 3:45 a.m. on a Tuesday morning in the year of our Lord 2012. Here you are. And me. Again. So why can't you just act like a normal not-insane person and go back to sleep? Huh? Dad's a bit tired, you see. Dad hasn't slept in two years. And now this is starting to feel a bit like going round, round, round in a car with your grandpa, do you understand that?

No, of course you don't. You don't get anything at all. But your dad has a headache now, so it would be super nice of you if you could at least use your inside voice if you have to get up and wreak havoc at a time of night not even strippers and drug dealers would consider as reasonable hours.

And yes. Dad can see that you're looking for the plastic giraffe. Dad knows you love that plastic giraffe. The one that dances all funny when you press a button on its back. And sings and plays "Oh My Darling" at the same time. Incredibly loudly. Every time you accidentally nudge it with your foot. Like fifteen minutes ago, for example, just after Dad got you back to sleep in your bed after a seven-hour miniature Mixed Martial Arts exhibition through the whole damn apartment, and Dad was just about to turn off the light and go back through the living room to Dad's bedroom. And that bastard was on the floor. And Dad tripped over it. And the music woke you up and you flew out of bed and roared, "RAFFE!!!"

Dad knows you loved Raffe.

And it's not as though Dad has . . . you know . . . killed Raffe. Or anything. Dad would never do that to someone you love.

But Raffe had to move, you see. Raffe lives on a very nice farm out in the countryside now. It's better there. Plastic giraffes love farms.

And I know you'll wonder why. But your mother became . . . allergic, you see. You'll have to take it up with her.

Can we go back to bed now? Please?

Because, you know, it's not that I don't

love spending this amount of quality time with you. Please understand that. I just kind of wish a little more of the quality was saved for a time of day when there's something good on TV. And it's not that I long for the time before you were born. Absolutely not! I'm just saying that, you know, I slept more back then. And I like sleeping. I'm good at it. I like sleep and sleep likes me. When your mother and I first met, one of our favorite things was to wake up on a Sunday morning, look at one another, crawl back under the covers, and doze off again. Sometimes, I would get up and make coffee just so I could go back to bed and wake up in an apartment that smelled of freshly brewed coffee.

Good times.

And then one morning, there you were, and one morning a year or so later, you learned to climb out of your crib and woke me up by wrapping your hands around my wrist and hitting me in the face with my own watch. Like the sixth-graders did when I first started middle school. "Ahahaha! Why are you hitting yourself? Look at Fredrik hitting himself! Harhar! Why are you hitting yourself?" That's what you do, you little bully. Why do you do that? What's your problem?

And then I have to get up and play with your train set or whichever piece of crap toy you've decided absolutely can't wait until morning. And it's just as well to get it over and done with, because you won't give in. It's like living with a tiny, tiny telemarketer. And I know I'm supposed to be the fun-loving great dad who plays on your level and still has a childish side and all that. But seriously. You're absolutely useless at playing with the train set. I'm not saying that to destroy your self-confidence or anything, it's just a bit of objective, constructive criticism. You stink at playing with trains. Someone has to tell you.

First of all, you're driving the train in the wrong direction. Where's the realism in that? And if we're not basing this game on reality, then why even play with a train? If we're just going to make stuff up and play without any borders of imagination, might we not just as well go the whole way with it? Then I want trolls and giants and unicorns that shoot at the trolls with golden slingshots out of their butts! But no, you're all "I'm wild and crazy, I'm driving the train BACKWARD!"

Seriously.

If we're playing trains, we're playing trains. And there's a right way and a wrong way. That's all I'm saying. So put the horse back in the dining car. (Yes, I know that your mother says that's not right. But honestly, what kind of car would you have a horse in if it's not in the dining car?) And stop looking so angry. The train is standing still in the tunnel right now because there's a signaling failure. "Technical problems." You're just going to have to accept that. And then the train needs to proceed to the next station incredibly, incredibly slowly because there are leaves on the tracks, you see. But if you like, I can be the train company and you can be the government department responsible for maintaining the infrastructure, and we can play that we're blaming one another in the media after some passengers froze to death in the tunnel. It'll be fun!

You see? This is working out great. We're bonding here, you and I.

Well, until you start pulling all the people out of the train and running around trying to shove them into your toy cars, that is. Have you never heard of climate change? I swear, sometimes it's like you don't give a damn about your environmental footprint at all! And then I have to put all the people back in the train later on, and you've lost all their luggage, and it'll be a nightmare of lawsuits! Where are you going?

What now? Are you angry?

Wait! Is this because you didn't understand my pop culture references when I sang Soul Asylum?

Fine! All right, then! It's three forty-five in the morning and Dad hasn't slept since you were born, but of course *y-o-u* are the real victim here! Is that it? If those vampires from *Twilight* had taken a single look at Dad right now, they would have mumbled, "Don't drink that one's blood, Edward, it looks sick." But let's feel sorry for you, shall we?

Fine. No more trains. Then can we go to bed?

Please?

No but seriously, now.

Pretty please?

I don't think you realize how much Dad is looking forward to you being old enough to understand the monetary system, so Dad can give you a hundred bucks for keeping quiet and letting Dad sleep. Dad can't do this anymore. Dad still doesn't know if your preschool teacher is going to report him to the police for asking at what age, roughly, she thought it was reasonable to start shooting kids with tranquilizer darts. People talk about "scientific sleeping methods for babies," but we're way past that here. Dad is reading a very nice book about how wildlife hunters in Australia take down freshwater crocodiles, you see.

And you know, another thing: I don't really trust your preschool teacher. She's a strange one. I once saw her go into a room with sixteen two-year-olds and she looked at all of you and said, "Sleep." And then you SLEPT! Like she was in the frikkin' X-Men!

Not cool, ma'am. Not cool.

Wait, where are you going now? We're going to bed! No, don't grab the toy cars now, because Dad will cry. "Have kids," they said. "It'll be fun," they said. Yeah, fun like trying to calm down a flock of panic-stricken antelopes using a stroboscope. Why do children hate sleeping? Why? Do you know I read in a magazine that children stay awake with the parent they like most, in order to keep them in the room for as long as possible? I would have gone to the office of that magazine and punched the writer of that article straight in the face if I wasn't so EXHAUSTED, all right?

Because we both know you like your mother most. I do too. She's the best thing to ever happen to either of us. And that's actually the biggest reason you need to be quiet.

Because I can take this, the fact that you and I are up all night. Honestly. I can take the scorching-hot bottles of formula and the goddamn plastic giraffes and the fact that we apparently HAVE to line up all the stuffed animals in exact size order before even considering bedtime. I get a bit sleep deprived, so I get migraines and forget things and park in the wrong space in the garage and stand in the stairwell once in a while swearing at the incompetent bastards who installed the locks in our buildings until the neighbor opens the door and wonders why I'm trying to break into their apartment. And sometimes I get the formula and the protein shakes mixed up. And ONCE when you were taking a nap, I got the bedroom door and the balcony door mixed up and put you to bed on the outdoor furniture instead. But I got you in after fifteen minutes and it was only November and you were mostly fine and no one will ever know or call social services or anything as long as I never write any of this down in a book.

I can take it. I don't have to sleep. I just don't want you to wake your mother. Agreed?

Because . . . honestly? This is one of the very few concrete things I can actually do for you and for her. Yeah, I know that sounds pathetic. But she does so much more than me. With our lives. With you. With us. And, at the very least, I want to be able to give her this in return.

She's just endlessly better at being a parent than I am. She understands exactly what you mean when you're standing in the hallway shouting and rambling incomprehensibly like a drunk Ewok. She knows what kind of clothes you should wear when it's cold out. She keeps track of papers from the doctor and makes sure we have vitamins and leans forward and kisses my neck long before I even realize myself how much I need her to do that precisely right then. There are so many fantastic sides of her that you haven't even gotten to know yet. That you aren't old enough to understand. And, oh, how you're going to love getting to know her. Her nooks and crannies and small secret corners and winding corridors and creaking closet doors. The way she lives every single feeling in her body to eternity and back.

The way she loves us: all in.

She might scream at us once in a while when we sit on the new sofa without pants on or when we leave wet towels on the bathroom floor. When we spill mayonnaise on the carpet and drop ice cream into her handbag. But your mother would stand in front of a pack of wolves for you and for me. It's an incomprehensible blessing to get to be her boys. We need to make sure we deserve it. Every single day.

Because when you're with her, it's always Sunday morning.

And the ONE thing in life I'm better at than she is is handling a lack of sleep. I park in the wrong space when I'm tired, but she drives to the wrong job when she is. When I've had a rough night she finds the cheese in the freezer, but when she's had a rough night I find the fridge in the basement. She's better at absolutely everything else, but just after you were born we noticed that this was one area where I was more high functioning than she was. The only one.

So, we need to give her this, you and I. For all the things she does for us every day, we need to give her this. We need to let her sleep at night so she can be all our Sunday mornings when she wakes up.

I hope you get that.

That's why we're sitting here watching cartoons and playing with your train set. Again. And Dad knows that Dad is an ass sometimes but Dad is just . . . tired. But Dad is trying. Really trying. Because Dad loves you. And yes, Dad is sorry for that thing with Raffe. Dad knows you loved Raffe. And Dad LOVES you. But Raffe is in a better place now. Or at least Dad is in a better place, because Raffe is in another place. Because there are limits, you know?

At three forty-five in the morning, there are limits.

I really want to be good at this. I just really want to be the kind of dad who can put his child to sleep. I want to be the good kind of dad. I don't want to fail you.

And at three forty-six, when you fall asleep with your little head heavy on my arm and that red toy engine in your hand, that's why I'm lying awake here, staring at you.

Sometimes, when I was quite small, your grandpa and I would go out in the car together. Round, round, round we would drive. I don't really know where we were going. Things needed picking up. Things needed dropping off. We never said all that much. We probably didn't even talk much at all when I was small, your grandpa and I. And when I got older, I used to think those car trips must have been incredibly boring. We just sat there next to one another in silence and drove, you know?

It was not until after you were born that I realized those were probably some of the very best moments of my childhood, for both me and your grandpa. Because they were ours.

And when you're all grown up, I guess it'll be the memory of nights like this that I'll hold most dear. I won't remember the headaches and the swearing then. I'll remember the trains. I'll remember when you worked out how to open the freezer and sat inside your play tent throwing ice cubes at me when I tried to get you into bed. How you made me laugh so hard that my very bones sang when you wanted me to chase you, and we ran through the entire apartment and ended up with you hiding inside a suitcase in the wardrobe having no idea how to get back out again. And then, when I set you free, you dropped an ice cube inside my T-shirt for the very first time. Your expression then. That laugh. That's what I'll remember. Those hours were ours.

And Raffe.

The stuff you remember from a childhood.

They really are the strangest of things.

THE ART OF CHOOSING YOUR WORK
ASSIGNMENTS

When your mother and I clean the apartment, I could take the easy, cowardly way out. You know that. I know that. But are we those kind of men, you and I? I say no.

So when it's Apartment Cleaning Day, I roll up my pants, take off my shirt, and walk straight into the most difficult-to-clean room without fear. No hesitation.

Yes. You heard me. I choose the bathroom. Voluntarily. I fall on that grenade. Because that's the kind of man I am. I'm not afraid.

And you should know that I don't just "clean" that bathroom. Any clown from the street can "clean" a bathroom. But I elevate cleaning to an art, a craftsmanship that has been passed down from Backman man to Backman man for generations. A tender skill. Some might even say it's a calling.

You don't become a magnificent bathroom cleaner. You're born one.

I start by removing any loose objects. Nothing that might shake loose under a high-pressure wash will be tolerated when my dictatorship over the kingdom the ignorant public call "the restroom" begins. Because a hero never "rests."

After that, I scrub the tiles with three different types of detergents. I wipe the mirror until the mirror's mirror image has its own damn mirror image. I rub the metal faucets with toothpaste until you can't even look at them without permanently damaging your eyes. I scrub the shower so meticulously that the International Olympic Committee submits an application to hold figure skating competitions there.

I clean the inside of the cupboard beneath the sink. I scour the waste pipes. I scrape the rubber molding with a toothbrush. I make Mr. Clean look so weak he'll turn himself in to the health department, *do you hear me?*

And once I'm done with all that, do you know what I do then? Do you? I do it all again. Just to make sure!

Once I'm finished with the shower, it's so shiny that a flock of crows tries to steal it. And when I'm finally done, when it's all over, when I step out of the bathroom like a soldier victorious from battle, when I return from the galactic showdown that is cleaning as done by not just a man but a Backman man, do you know what happens then? Then I find your mother in the living room. The woman I live and die for. And she looks at me and says:

"Oh, great! Just great! While you've been in the *shower* for three and a half hours,

I've cleaned the entire apartment *on my own*! Do you know how unfair that is, Fredrik?!"

I'm Not Saying It's the *Only* Reason I Love Her.

We're waiting to order takeout in a restaurant and a group of middle-aged men in too-large blazers and Bluetooth headsets cuts in line.

And I get annoyed. And your mother tells me not to cause a scene. And I get even more annoyed.

And one of the middle-aged men turns around. Sees us. Meets your mother's eye, now clearly aware that they've cut before us in line. And then he quickly turns back and pretends like nothing's happened.

And I tap him on the shoulder. And he ignores me. And I want to hit him. And your mother forbids me.

And then she takes out her phone and goes out into the street and makes a call. And when she comes back in again someone shouts, "Number sixty-four!" from behind the counter. And your mother says, "Here!" and elbows past the entire line and takes the food and pays. And on the way back out, she looks each of the middle-aged men in the eye and smiles.

And I look at her and say, "Did you just call the restaurant to order food while we were standing in line?"

And she shrugs in surprise and says,

"Doesn't everyone?"

I'm not saying it's the only reason I love her.

But it really doesn't hurt.

I'M NOT SAYING YOU SHOULD LOVE DAD MORE THAN MOM. OF COURSE NOT. I'M JUST PRESENTING THE FACTS.

"Nothing with swords." Nothing. With. Swords.

What kind of person sits down with her loving family on New Year's Day to watch a movie and says something like that?

And can she be trusted?

Just ask yourself that.

What You Need to Know about Why That Felicia Girl's Mother Hates Me

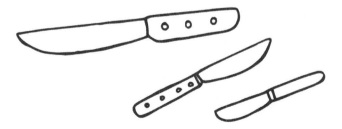

Yes. I know you like that Felicia girl. But the fact is that Felicia's mother happens to think your dad is a bit of an idiot, all right? So we probably won't be playing with her so much in the near future.

You look like you want an explanation.

Well, first of all, let me just say that this whole parenting thing isn't actually as damn easy as it looks. There's a lot of new things to take into consideration here. Like sugar, for example. People who look perfectly together on the outside can throw tantrums like angry art students if you talk about kids and sugar, did you know that? I'm serious: that time I happened to joke about you and me being home alone around Christmas when you were eighteen months old, sharing a large pitcher of "Scandinavian Health Inspection" (that's vodka and Dr Pepper; we'll talk about that when you're older). That William kid's father was actually more furious that I'd insinuated I'd given you soda than that I'd insinuated I'd given you alcohol.

I suppose it probably didn't help that I gave you your milk bottle in a brown paper bag over the next few days.

And it *definitely* didn't help that your mother couldn't stop herself from telling one of the other parents, "It's for his dead homies," when you spilled it. (So this is also largely her fault!)

But I'm not trying to pass the blame here. I'm not saying it was easier being a parent fifty years ago or anything like that. Only, I do think the rules of play were a bit clearer back then. It's just hard to know what's socially acceptable and not nowadays. When you were around six months old, for example, a nurse told us that we shouldn't let you "sleep for too long in the afternoon, because there's a risk of disruption to his circadian rhythms." Apparently, it was then perfectly fine for your mother to say, "Well, it's not just a case of 'waking' a child who seems to go into the cryosleep from *Avatar* whenever he closes his eyes." The nurse even laughed at that.

But apparently it was not at all okay for me to add, "Yeah, yeah, like, seriously! Not even prison guards with the security cameras turned off could figure out a way to keep this kid awake!" That was not okay at all.

Do you see what I mean? It's not easy to know where the boundaries are sometimes.

And you know when the same nurse explained, on your next checkup, that it was good to wean children off eating at night at this age, and suggested "different methods for reducing appetite," I wondered aloud whether they meant we should teach you to smoke or something. That was wrong too.

There are a lot of unwritten parent rules here. You're meant to be a good role model. You aren't meant to swear. You should know that it's called a "playpen" and not an "octagon." And that when the preschool teachers refer to something as "nature's own candy," they almost always mean raisins and almost never bacon. And that when other parents with small children talk about children and TV and kindly but firmly inform you that "there is actually research" that proves exactly how damaging TV is for small children, they really do mean all TV. Not just *bad* TV. *All* TV.

Including *Game of Thrones*.

Even now, I'm still not entirely sure where we stand with this whole thing when the nurse asked if we had "any other health questions" and I took the opportunity to ask at what age you can normally tell whether a child is right- or left-footed. And the nurse asked, "Why?" And I said, "To know if he's a left winger or a right winger." I think that was all right. But it's not all that easy to know. The nurse mostly talked to your mother after that.

Social limitations and pop culture references become slightly blurred when you fraternize after reproduction. The fact that Po from *Teletubbies* actually sports a pretty provocative camel toe for the majority of the entire second season, you'd think that would be a perfect icebreaker during the introductions at the parent-teacher conference at preschool, right?

But no.

So I'm sorry for all of this.

Truly.

Being a good parent is hard. There's a lot of trial and error. In my case, quite a lot of the latter. I joke compulsively when I'm criticized, you probably know that already, it's a character flaw. And one thing you're never lacking once you become a parent is people criticizing you. Because children aren't just children these days, you know, you're identity markers. No one knows quite how that happened. Ten thousand years of sexual experience, and suddenly my generation decides that we're going to carry you out of the maternity ward as though you were the Stanley Cup. As though we were the first people in the history of the world who figured out how reproduction works.

We don't even need to be "good" parents anymore, I think. That's passed now. We make do with "not horrible" by this point. All we want is for your psychologists to mutter, in twenty years' time, that it might not be *e-n-t-i-r-e-l-y* our fault.

And one of the few ways we can convince ourselves that we're actually decent as parents is by making other people seem like bad parents. And we can be pretty damn creative when it comes down to it, I'll have you know. If it isn't the food or the toys or the fact that the child sometimes has to stay at preschool until quarter past three in the afternoon (QUARTER PAST THREE!!! I might as well have just left you in the woods and let the WOLVES raise you!!!) then it's the nonorganic plastic in whatever the hell piece of furniture that hasn't been given some certificate by some department in Brussels. "Oh? You let your child play with THAT? Ah, well, me personally, I would rather my child didn't get brain cancer . . . but it's nice that everyone can raise their children in their own way, isn't it?" That's how we bring each other down.

We find some poor bastard who doesn't realize that if you don't wash all children's clothes at nine thousand degrees before they're worn for the first time, then the child will develop mutated allergies and die. As though that's how mankind has evolved to be the dominant species on Earth. As though we lived in caves and wrapped newborns in mammoth skin, and if the mammoth skin wasn't dry-cleaned first, then the kid died. As though that as how we survived on a planet where not even the dinosaurs could handle the pressure.

And if it's not that, then it's something else. If we can't make one another look bad by caring a little more, then we do it by caring a little less. That's when people, out of sheer obstinacy, are transformed into those cool, relaxed parents with sunglasses and lower-back tattoos and coffee in paper cups and books about "free-range parenting" sticking out of their canvas tote bags, who are all "Children must be allowed to be chiiiildren, y'know what I mean? Just chill out, yeah?" While their five-year-old ray of sunshine with a Mohawk and a nose piercing tries to jam his little sister into a beer bottle in the background.

Or it's one of those idiot fathers at a dinner party who sits there all self-important and superior while the other parents joke about how at Christmas their kids would rather play with the cardboard box than with whatever was inside it. And someone laughs that "next Christmas I'll just buy them a huge box!" and everyone but that one father giggles hysterically. And someone else blurts out that their child will only play with the Tupperware in the kitchen cupboard. And everyone but that idiot father thinks it hilarious.

And then someone happily turns to that father to ask whether *his* child has any of those funny, unexpected things they like to play with, and then of course he has to be so damn special and difficult and antiestablishment, so he replies: "Mmm. Knives."

I'm not saying that I'm that father.

But that story might be partly why you aren't allowed to play with Theodor or Smilla anymore.

So anyway: it's not as easy as it looks, this whole being-a-parent thing, you know? I do the best I can. I go to the playground. I talk to other parents. I shake my head and cry, "Nooooo!?" when they tell me about some other parent of some other kid who erupted green stuff from their rectum or some other crap I couldn't really care less about if I tried. (Believe me, I've tried incredibly hard and I couldn't do it.) And I do actually try to be attentive. Sensitive. Empathetic. I get just as heated up over the scandals around the swine flu vaccine and the lack of qualified teachers and all that other stuff, the fact that there was some kind of poison or something in the walls of your preschool and that we had to be super careful to remember something when we did something or whatever the hell it was. I'm doing the best I can! It's just that I have a lot to think about.

And this thing everyone says about how you "don't become interested in children until you have them yourself," that's actually a lie. I only became interested in one (1) child when you were born. I still think other children are pretty annoying.

And yes. I know it's usually me who's the problem. That I don't listen and that I don't take things seriously.

Like when there was that health scare in the papers about bacteria-infested hot dogs that could be dangerous for children. And that Felicia girl's mother was really agitated that the preschool couldn't guarantee they wouldn't be serving the hot dogs on field trips. Or anywhere else. Ever. And I asked what the health risks from these hot dogs actually were, and Felicia's mother hissed, "Meningitis!" And I said, "Worth it!" And she got very, very angry.

Sure.

Maybe I shouldn't have suggested Felicia's mother should "have a Prozac and a drink and try to be a bit more *hakuna matata.*" I probably shouldn't have.

And a few weeks later, when she was a bit wound up during winter about the vomiting bug and was very insistent that the children shouldn't touch one another, not even one another's clothes. And it was that morning when you woke me up by hitting me in the face with a small toy car, so I had a nosebleed. And I thought I'd managed to stop it. And then we got to preschool. And I sneezed in the cloakroom.

I shouldn't have sneezed in the cloakroom.

So. Well. You know.

I know you like that Felicia girl.

But things are what they are.

IT WAS JUST A SUGGESTION.

All right. So it was last night. 11:30 p.m.

I was very, very, very tired. And you were running around, around, around on the floor and shouting something that sounded like the sort of thing drunk German soccer hooligans would shout to each other when really happy. And then you just stopped. Rushed into the kitchen. Came back. Got yourself into position and then started, with what I can only describe as an impressively indifferent facial expression, to pour yogurt into a drawer. No explanation at all.

And all I said then was that you usually fall asleep when we go for a drive in the car. And then your mother's friend, who was visiting, laughed and said yeah, but then they sadly always wake up when you get back home and have to take them out of the car seat.

And then I said that I'm pretty damn sure that baby monitor we bought would have reception all the way down to the garage.

It was a joke. It was mostly a joke. At least a little bit of it was not serious.

But if someone from social services turns up at preschool today and starts asking questions about this, you know what it's about.

THE COBBLER'S CHILDREN

I'm not saying it wasn't my fault.

I'm just saying that this whole process of getting a child's outerwear on in the morning is a bit like trying to put an angry monkey who has just been dipped in soap and fed jalapeños into a complete ice hockey goalkeeper's uniform.

I'm not making excuses.

I'm just saying that things were a bit stressful this morning.

And it's not like you walk all the way to preschool either. You get pushed in a bloody stroller. Sitting inside an enormous fur blanket zipped up around you like a frikkin' sleeping bag. There's not a single person in the entire Stockholm area who had a warmer commute to work this morning than you. That's just how it is.

That's not an excuse.

I'm just saying.

But sure.

Sure. Sure. Sure. Fine.

When it's two below outside and I lift you up and out of the stroller outside preschool, in front of half a dozen other parents and all the staff, and then put you down straight into a pile of snow. And it takes me maybe about thirty or so seconds before I realize you aren't wearing any shoes.

Then that doesn't make me look like the most competent of parents. I get that.

But I'm having a bit of a day.

NOTE TO SELF

Men coming back to work from paternity leave *don't* like it if you welcome them back from their "vacation."

■ ■ ■ ■

WHAT YOU NEED TO KNOW ABOUT GOOD AND EVIL

■ ■ ■ ■

There are those who say that no one is born evil. There are even those who say that there aren't any evil people at all. I'm not an academic, so I can't give you a definite truth on the matter. All I know is that there are bastards. And that, if possible, I would really like it if you did not grow up to become one of them.

Because if there's just one thing I really wish I could teach you, it's to be kind. To not be a jerk. And you can trust me on this particular subject, because I have very extensive experience of being a jerk. I've got a PhD in behaving like an ass.

So this is one of the very basic things you need to know about how the world works: in every group you'll ever find yourself in, regardless of whether it's on a playground or in the office of an advertising agency with panoramic windows, you'll meet people who constantly place those around them into two groups: the strong and the weak.

But between these two groups there will be a gap, and in this gap there will be ten other people. The most dangerous group. Terrified of tumbling down the hierarchy. And those ten will always hit and kick downward because that's the only direction in which they know how to hit and kick. They'll always find an excuse, any at all, to push someone weaker than them into a corner.

And I'm just like every other parent. I'm terrified you'll be the child in the corner of the playground. Equally terrified you'll be the one being hit and that you'll be the one doing the hitting. I've been both, and it hurts in different places but in the same way.

So you and I need to talk about good and evil. Because that's the kind of thing fathers do with their sons, I think. I just don't have the slightest idea where to start, to be honest. So I want to tell you a story. Because you like stories, right? Everybody does.

Now, I don't happen to know a huge number of stories, so I'll tell you one of the few I do know. The one I liked the very best when I was a kid. And I want you to focus on the moral of it. Because the moral is important.

Let's begin: Once upon a time, there was

a wrestler called The Undertaker.

The Undertaker lived a long, long time ago in a kingdom far, far away called the United States. Like, all the way back in the nineties. And in this kingdom, what all the wrestlers wanted most of all was to wrestle in the big WWE competition in front of thousands of people and defeat an opponent with really bad hair and get to wear the golden champion's belt. And year after year, for as long as the people could remember, the evil kings Bret Hart and Shawn Michaels dominated these competitions. Some even said they were invincible. But when The Undertaker stepped into the ring for the first time, oh, you should have seen him then! He gave the people hope that a better day might dawn. He was a hero in a world of villains. Big as a tractor, this guy. And he had a finisher that . . . sorry, wait. Maybe we should start from the beginning? A "finisher" is a signature way of knocking out your opponent, you see. All the wrestlers had one back then. It was the kind of thing you learned at wrestling school. It's a punch or a choke hold so strong that there's no comeback to it. Like a tank. Or a tank shooting fire. Or a full stop, the end, no givesies backsies jinx.

You know what I mean? Nothing beats no

givesies backsies jinx.

So: The Undertaker had a finisher called "The Tombstone Piledriver," where he sort of turned his opponent upside down. Your mother is fairly insistent that you might not need to know all the details about this right now. And maybe she's right. You've got plenty of time to learn. But just imagine you had something stuck in your throat and that I turned you upside down to shake it out, and then I happened to drop you. That's pretty much what The Undertaker did. But on purpose.

It was aaawesooome!

He was fated to become the WWE champion. (That's, like, the wrestling equivalent of "the princess and half the kingdom.") Everyone loved The Undertaker. He was tall, dark, and handsome, and he had biceps as big as Labrador puppies. But! Beneath the glittering surface, he carried a dark secret. And one day, a shadow from his past reemerged: his half brother, Kane.

You see, Kane's parents had died in a terrible fire, and everyone thought that Kane did too. But they were wrong. He was left with serious burns to his face, but he survived. And he grew bitter and angry, and some really bad people who wanted to hurt him lied and said that it was his brother,

The Undertaker, who started the fire, in an attempt to kill Kane. So Kane, filled with hate, swore that one day he would take his revenge. And then, just as The Undertaker fought Shawn Michaels in the deciding match to determine who would face Bret Hart in a spectacular to-the-death fight for the WWE belt, Kane suddenly turned up and challenged his brother in front of the entire kingdom. (Not to mention TV viewers in up to sixty-three countries.)

But The Undertaker didn't want to fight his brother. And so he did what everyone will tell you to do if someone hits you: he walked away. And there's no shame in that. Kane stood there shouting, "Chicken!" after him, but he was wrong. Because it was Kane who was the chicken. Never forget that.

The Undertaker refused to raise his fists to his own brother. But Kane, like all bullies, wouldn't give in. He mocked and humiliated The Undertaker. He called him "coward" and "weakling" and a load of other words that . . . well, you'll understand once you're older but that, simply put, relate to the different ways boys and girls pee. Kane declared that he would get his revenge sooner or later and then he continued to turn up at all The Undertaker's fights, challenging him to a duel. He even jumped into the ring and started to fight on a number of occasions, but The Undertaker just took his blows without so much as raising a pinkie finger in defense. Even though maybe The Undertaker SHOULD have!

You get where I'm going?

I mean . . . I'm not telling you to beat up your sibling. I know that might be how it sounds right now. And when I think about it, maybe this wasn't the best example. But what I'm trying to say is that sometimes the strongest person isn't the one who hits. It's the one who doesn't hit back. All right?

You see: The Undertaker could have crushed Kane, but he chose to be bigger than that. And at some point in time, in a playground or in an office with panoramic windows at an advertising agency, I hope you'll realize that the brave person isn't the one who starts a fight even though he doesn't know whether he'll win or lose. The brave person is the one who knows he would win and still holds back.

But we're getting off track here. So: Kane tried and tried to get his brother to fight him, but The Undertaker refused. He just walked away, every time. And time passed. And, just like in every great fairy tale, Kane eventually realized his mistake. He understood that he had been wrong all along, that

162

blood is thicker than water. And so, at one of the kingdom's wrestling events one dark night, when The Undertaker was ambushed by Shawn Michaels and his three shady villain sidekicks from D-Generation X, Kane rushed to his brother's aid. To begin with, Shawn Michaels naturally assumed that Kane would join in on their side, because that's what all bullies think. That just because there are more of them and because they're attacking a lone victim, no one will dare stand up to them. And sadly, I'm not going to lie to you, people like Shawn Michaels are often right. That's why the bullies continue to be bullies, because they win so often. But not this time. My oh my.

Not. This. Time.

Kane rushed into the ring and picked up Shawn Michaels by the hair and choke-slammed him straight onto the floor, and all the D-Generation X bullies immediately ran away like scared rabbits.

It was one of the most beautiful sporting moments of my entire youth.

And the very next day, Kane and The Undertaker teamed up under the name "The Brothers of Destruction." And they became the most feared and unbeatable warriors in the entire wrestling kingdom.

And everyone lived happily ever after.

■ ■ ■ ■

Until a few years later, when Kane betrayed his brother and choked him out in the 1998 Royal Rumble fight. And then Shawn Michaels helped him lock The Undertaker in a box. And then they set fire to the box.

But, I mean, that's not really the important part of the story. Focus on the moral of it.

The moral is that it's not always right to hit back. But that sometimes you have to, if you're defending the weakest.

Not that I'm saying you're allowed to fight, that is. Of course you aren't. Your mother would be angry as hell. So you're never allowed to fight. Other than with middle-aged Germans in sombreros when they cut in line to the breakfast buffet at hotels, of course. But everyone knows that. They're an exception. But otherwise: no fighting. Other than when you need to defend yourself. Or defend someone else. Or when someone tries to take the last chocolate waffle. But never other than that!

Well. This isn't going exactly the way I planned.

But, here: I just want you to know that I'm not going to try to trick you into thinking there's no evil in the world. Because there is. This world sometimes seems like it's full of incomprehensible, unintelligible, unembraceable, inexorable evil. Violence and injustice and greed and blind rage.

But it's also full of all that other stuff. The small things. Kindness between strangers. Love at first sight. Loyalty and friendship. Someone's hand in yours on a Sunday afternoon. Two brothers reconciled. Heroes who stand up when no one else dares. A fiftysomething man in a Saab who slows down when he sees your turn signal and lets you into his lane during rush hour. Summer nights. Children's laughter. Cheesecake.

And all you can do is decide which side you want to be on. Which pile you want to contribute to.

I won't always be the best father. I've made many mistakes, and I'll make plenty more. But I'll never forgive myself if you become that kid in the corner in the playground.

Whichever of them that is.

I was almost always one of those ten in the middle, terrified of ending up on the wrong side of the line. Sometimes I still am. Most of us are.

So be different from me, better, do me that favor. Never keep your mouth shut.

Don't look away. Never be mean just because you can be. Never mistake kindness for weakness. Don't become the kind of person who stands in an office with panoramic windows in an advertising firm and thinks that "nice" is an insult.

The Undertaker taught me that. I hope I can teach you the same.

And, yeah, maybe don't tell your mother what I said about Kane putting his brother into a box and setting it on fire. She doesn't understand wrestling.

ALL RIGHT. HERE'S WHAT HAPPENED.

Let's assume you're feeling a bit stressed and you spill milk on the diaper bag, and you think, "Damn, this is going to stink, I'll seem like the worst dad!" So instead you grab the first plastic bag you can find for carrying the diapers and spare clothes for your baby. And you throw all that into the stroller as you grab the garbage bags on your way out the door. And down by the trash cans, you pick them up and something from one of the garbage bags runs down your sleeve. And you're feeling a bit stressed, so you think, "It's probably just juice, it'll dry." And then you grab the first thing you can find to wipe yourself down. And it just so happens to be a diaper from the bag you packed your baby's things into. And then you jump into a fairly warm car. And just as you do that, you notice that your baby needs changing. And then you think, "Ah, what the hell, I already have this diaper in my hand, a little juice won't hurt him!" and so you put the diaper you used to dry up what you thought was juice onto the baby. And then you drive. And twenty minutes later you arrive at preschool just in time for singing. Out of breath and red in the face. With a shopping bag from the local liquor store full of diapers. And your car keys in one hand. And a child that smells like warm beer in the other.

When that happens, let's just say that the option of using a diaper bag with a few milk stains on it suddenly seems like a pretty attractive alternative. From a purely good parent–bad parent perspective, that is.

Let's assume that.

WHY IT'S NOT WORTH ARGUING
WITH YOUR MOTHER

I wonder who takes a bottle of Schweppes Bitter Lemon from the kitchen counter, pours it out, refills the bottle with water and dish soap, puts it in the sink, and goes to bed.

Your mother wonders who gets up in the morning, sees a bottle full of what he thinks is ten-hour-old lukewarm soda, and drinks it.

I wonder who the hell doesn't realize that dish soap and water will look exactly like a bottle of nicely room-temperature Schweppes Bitter Lemon at ten past six in the morning.

Your mother wonders who the hell would drink from a bottle of yesterday's soda in the sink first thing they do at ten past six in the morning.

I wonder what kind of moron puts dish soap into a bottle.

Your mother says that at least she isn't the moron who just drank dish soap.

She wins.

THE ART OF TALKING TO STRANGERS

Here are two things we apparently need to stop doing when strangers bend down over your stroller to look at how cute you are:

1. Me sneaking up behind the stroller, hissing, "Say hello to my little FRIEND!"
2. Me sneaking up behind the stroller, hissing, "Dance, puppets. Daaance!"

So. Yeah. This is mostly feedback to me.

You just carry on.

■ ■ ■ ■

WHAT YOU NEED TO KNOW ABOUT STARTING A BAND

■ ■ ■ ■

So, son, let me explain to you that all this that you see around you right now is called "life." It's going to be complicated at times and it's going to demand certain things of you. You'll need to be honest and brave and just. Love and be loved. Fail. Embarrass yourself. Triumph. Fall from something. Fall for someone.

And you'll need to start a band. I might as well say that right now. And the first thing you'll need is a good name.

Sure, there are people who will say rubbish like "the music has to come first," but honestly, those people's music is always rubbish. A good name always comes first. Like "The Who" or "The Smiths" or "Nuns with Guns" or "Draco and the Malfoys." Quality band names, every one of them. My friend R was in a cover band called "Stiff Nipples" for a short time. Not quite as good but also not entirely bad.

I myself have always dreamed of having a power metal band called "Frightening Lightning." On the T-shirts, all the *i*'s would be lightning bolts. That's really the most important thing to know about starting a band: that the name should look good on T-shirts. In Frightening Lightning, my friend R would be in charge of speakers, my friend D in charge of the tour bus, my friend J the cords and cables, my friend E would be in charge of getting gas station hot dogs, and I would be in charge of T-shirts. Your mother, of course, keeps claiming that T-shirts aren't "real instruments," but honestly: your mother doesn't know the first thing about music.

The second most important thing about starting a band is that you do it with your best friends. There are moments in life where someone might try to make you question why a modern man in a high-technology society needs a best friend. But your mother buys a lot of crap from eBay. And we move basically every third year. That's a lot of stuff that needs to be carried. And, what the hell, sometimes you just want someone to play video games with. A best friend is good to have.

There aren't really any fundamental requirements for that, of course. But since we're already on the subject, let's establish a few all the same: A real friend won't steal your crush. A real friend won't ninja loot your warrior in World of Warcraft.

Yeah, that's basically it.

You can have a best friend like Ron in *Harry Potter.* But, well, you know. He whines a lot, doesn't he? It's worthless. Plus he steals Hermione, the bastard. No, it's better to have a best friend who's like Chewbacca in *Star Wars.* He's more the kind all your crushes think is cute and a good listener, but who they just want to be friends with. Man-At-Arms from *He-Man* is a quality choice too, because he won't ever judge you, no matter who your crush is.

Or you could have one like Goose in *Top Gun.* Although he dies. And that's honestly a terrible character trait in a best friend. If I'd had the chance to choose, I probably would have gone for someone like Samwise Gamgee.

Say what you like about Samwise Gamgee in *The Lord of the Rings,* but Samwise Gamgee would damn well never steal your stuff in World of Warcraft!

Plus, I think Samwise would have been a good rhythm guitarist. Chewbacca's more of a drummer. Man-At-Arms is a keyboardist. Ron Weasley probably plays bass, the bastard. The bass player always steals all your crushes. And yeah, Goose is dead. So he doesn't play anything. Other than dead, that is.

Not everyone will understand why you need to have a band. I'm not going to name names. Partly because I don't want to single anyone out and partly because you already know your mother's name. But she doesn't get this. Always moaning about why I "can't just go for a coffee like a normal person" and how I "can't spend time with other men without having some kind of activity associated with it." It's all lies, of course. I don't need an activity to be able to hang out with other men. I just think it's nice to have something to do while you're together. Plus, being in a band is cool. It could be a rock band. Or a pop band. Or a cover band. As long as it's something where you can gather around and look at one another and say, "But you know, when the band makes it big . . ."

And yes. The band will probably never make it even out of our storage unit. And, to be completely honest, it actually doesn't even need to be a band. It could be a football team we'll never get around to starting or a bar we'll never buy or a perfect bank robbery we'll never carry out. (That's partly because we don't want to go to prison, but mostly because none of us really knows where to get hold of the bag of automatic weapons, an amphibious car, four empty oxygen tanks, a dozen parachutes made of Ziploc bags, a man-size jar of honey, and six robot sharks and the rest of the stuff we need for our plan, but that's a different story entirely.)

Sometimes, it's just nice to go someplace where people care about a good T-shirt, that's all. So you need a best friend. Someone who knows who you were when you were fifteen. Someone you don't need to explain everything to. Someone you can drink whiskey and lie with. Someone you can call up and say, "Want to watch the game tonight?" Or "I was thinking of test-driving a car over the weekend, want to come along and finish all of my sentences with 'that's what SHE said!'?"

Or "Heyyyy, so my wife bought another secondhand sofa online and they don't have an elevator, so I was thinking . . ."

It's not like I have an activity for every friend. I'm not a freak. Some of them have the same activity. You have your Champions League friends. A few video game friends. While you're growing up, you'll have friends you only ever play poker with and friends you only ever go to the pub with. My friend N and I share an office. My friend J and I mostly tell jokes and watch *Family Guy.* My friend B and I talk about money and politics. My friend R and I call one another and talk for hours about all the stuff people talk about, kids and work and love and things you dream about and things that scare the shit out of you. He was the best man at my wedding. He's been my best man since we were fifteen.

My friend E and I? We eat. And by that, I don't mean we go to vineyards in Provence and sample crackers. I mean we eat sandwiches. And kebabs. And gas station hot dogs. It's E who taught me that no gas station hot dog on Earth is better than the mustard you put on it. A few years ago, the very best gas station hot dogs on Earth were found at a small gas station in the very southernmost part of Sweden; E still refers to them as "the first *Godfather* movie of gas station hot dogs" with a dreamy look in his eyes.

And, sure, sometimes you'll probably want a friend who can back you up in a fight or cross the North Pole with you. But much more often, you'll want a friend who'll just go with you to grab a burger on a Tuesday evening, so you don't have to be the lonely guy in the burger joint on a Tuesday evening. E's that kind of guy.

You just have different kinds of friends when you grow up. Some you play tennis with and some you party with and some you run around town and get into fights with. I used to have one I just drove around listening to music with. He died in a car accident when I was twenty. E took the day off work and drove forty miles just to give me a ride to the funeral. "I'm not good at talking about death," he mumbled, looking down at the wheel. "It's fine," I said, getting out. Once the funeral was over, he was there waiting for me with two kebabs. We ate them in his car. Then we drove around all night, listening to music and eating gas station hot dogs, because E didn't want me to go home and call the guys I only ever got drunk with. It's one of the nicest things anyone has ever done for me.

And then we got older. I moved to Stockholm. Met your mother. Got an apartment and a four-wheel drive. And you know what life is like. Though actually, you don't know yet. It's just that it's never like it was before. Suddenly, you don't have the time. You don't have the energy. You deprioritize one another. Become adults.

That's why you need a band. Just so you

have a reason once in a while to meet down in the recording studio (or "our friend Jimmie's mom's garage" in layman's terms). Not because the music itself is so important. But because all the rest of it is.

E eventually moved to Stockholm too. And I met N here. J and R and all the others stayed back home. Some of us live incredibly different lives now, and some of us live identical lives, only rarely beside one another. Some of us have even stopped listening to Rage Against the Machine. But every time we meet, we still spend a lot of time talking about the perfect band T-shirt. About the perfect song. The perfect guitar riff.

About perfect memories.

Like when we were nineteen and got incredibly drunk on R's birthday, and by the end of the evening E was bent double over the bar and R thought he wanted to say something, so he bent down with his head next to him so that he could hear over the music. And then E threw up in his ear. R still claims he has reduced hearing in that ear. That it's the reason he never became a better guitarist. "Acoustic feedback instability in the monitoring, you know?" (We don't know.)

I just want you to know you'll need something in your life that's never going to change.

So you'll need a band. If for nothing else than to be able to call them and say, "How's the new MacBook?" or "What the hell are A.C. Milan doing?" or "Want to come over for a barbecue?" without them getting hung up on details like it being November and you living in an apartment.

Or for asking for help moving a couch.

Or for swallowing hard and whispering, "She said yes."

Last year, E and I went to a little roadside bar in Ytterån, just outside of Östersund, way out in the north of Sweden. They have the biggest burger in the country there, nine and a half pounds. I guess people deal with their midlife crises in different ways. Some go climbing in the Himalayas, some cross the North Pole, and some take up martial arts. E and I? That burger was our Everest. There and back, it was eight hundred miles and fourteen hours of driving, just to eat lunch. On the way, we discussed what the very best "a man walks into a bar" joke was. We stopped at a gas station and ate hot dogs with strong mustard.

When I dropped E off outside his house that evening, we hugged. I can only remember us doing that once before. The day after you were born.

You weighed two pounds less than that burger.

So you'll need best friends. Frodo knew that. Han Solo knew that. He-Man and Maverick knew that. You need someone you can call when you need help moving that bloody bookcase. Or someone you can say "They should play Zlatan Ibrahimović in more of a drop-back position" to or "Have you found a good stream for the new *Game of Thrones* episode?"

Or "I'm going to be a dad."

You'll need a band.

THINKING OUTSIDE THE BOX

Your grandpa was here over the weekend and he installed those little child safety locks all over the kitchen.

The result is that it now takes you about fifteen seconds to get into a cupboard. And it takes me half an hour.

COMMUNICATION. IT'S THE KEY TO EVERY HEALTHY MARRIAGE.

ME: (*Looking out of the window*) You know that neighbor, the one with the big box on their balcony that you thought was an extra fridge?

MY WIFE: Yeah.

ME: That box is probably not a fridge.

MY WIFE: Huh?

ME: No. They have a rabbit in there.

MY WIFE: What? A rabbit? How do you know that?

ME: Because they have it out right now and they're playing with it.

MY WIFE: What do you mean playing with it?

ME: Well, they're cuddling and petting it.

MY WIFE: (*Sounding upset*) They've got a DEAD RABBIT in the fridge on their balcony and they're CUDDLING AND PETTING it?!

ME: For God's sake, honey. The rabbit's alive.

MY WIFE: (*Furious*) THEY HAVE A LIV-ING RABBIT IN THEIR FRIDGE???!!!

(*Silence*)

ME: You know, sometimes it feels like you don't listen to me at all.

EMPATHY. YOUR MOTHER HAS IT.
Dinner with a couple who have children your age

HER: (*Looking at the children playing on the floor*) God, they're so big already. I've almost forgotten all the bad things about being pregnant now.

HIM: Yeah, it's crazy how quickly you forget. You had a real tough time there for a while.

HER: Yeah, it's just that so much of it was new. So many weird things happening to my body.

YOUR MOTHER: No joke. My body went completely insane. I just waddled around all fat and clumsy, feeling like an elephant in everyone's way. I couldn't even fly properly. I'm used to being able to curl my feet up beneath me on the seat, but suddenly I barely had room for my legs! And let's not even get into how starving and cranky I was all the time, sweating constantly, the permanent heartburn . . .

(*Silence*)

YOUR MOTHER: I actually developed much more understanding for Fredrik afterward. He lives like that constantly.

185

WHAT YOU NEED TO KNOW ABOUT LOVE

I don't know all that much about love, if I'm completely honest.

I mean, I can tell you I love you, but I don't know if you understand what that really means. Because I don't love you the way I love bacon or Manchester United or the second season of *The West Wing.* This isn't that kind of love. I mean that I love you as though you were a runaway freight train thundering through every cell in my body. I mean that this love didn't grow on me, it knocked me over. It's an ongoing state of emergency.

But love. I don't know what to say about that. I don't know all that much about it. Of course I know that people say it's when you find someone who "completes" you, but honestly: I'm not so sure about that. When things are complete, that means they're in order. No joins or cracks. Just perfection. Two puzzle pieces cut precisely for one another. Like when you see two people and say, "God, those two were destined for each other!"

And, well. Your mother is from Tehran. I'm from the south of Sweden. She's five feet tall. I'm six foot one. If you put me on one side of a set of scales and two of her on the other, my side would still tip the balance. I lumber through life with my hands in my pockets; she dances. I don't actually know anything she loves doing as much as she loves dancing, and I can't find the rhythm in a clock. People have said lots of things about us, but trust me, no one has ever said that we were destined for each other.

So I don't know what to tell you about love. Maybe that some people say you need to know yourself before you can know anyone else. That could be true. I've put a great deal of time into getting to know myself, and that's given me a whole load of valuable insights. Like the fact that I know I love the second season of *The West Wing* and Manchester United. And bacon. Not the way I love you or your mother, of course. Not at all. I have a different kind of love for bacon. I don't know if you will too. Your mother always mutters that no one on Earth could love bacon the way I do. She often says that when other women travel for work they're afraid they'll find another woman's underwear on the bedroom floor when they get home, but she's expecting to find a defibrillator.

I don't know what you'll grow up to be. How much of me will end up a part of you. You have all her big brown eyes and her endless shadows on your cheeks. There are days when I think someone must have blown all her eyelashes into the ocean just to wish for you. You have all her laughter and all her spellbinding ability to step into a room and immediately make everyone in it want to move a little closer. Not like when I step into a room, and they instinctively hide all of the lasagna dishes and table decorations.

But if there's the slightest genetic hint of my side in that little body of yours, then you'll spend a large portion of the next ninety or so years being hungry. You may as well prepare yourself for that now. Life will revolve around food.

Thinking about food, dreaming about food, hunting for food, making food, ordering food, waiting for food, talking about food, questioning the lack of food. Never in my life have I looked at a menu and thought, "What looks nice?" I've always been too busy focusing on "What will be served in the largest portion?" If I ever write an autobiography, it'll be called *Hungry — A Lifestyle.*

Your mother likes different stuff. She understands beautiful things in a way I wish I could. Art, music, theater. Maybe I'm too focused on what kind of snacks there will be during the intermission to be able to maintain enough concentration for all that, I don't know. But I do lose focus pretty quickly. And my temper, I can lose that pretty easily too. Especially when I'm hungry. It's had quite an impact on my life.

So at roughly the same time your mother and I moved in together, she introduced the concept of "pre-eating" to me for anytime we were going anywhere with what she refers to as "grown adults" present. By "grown adults," she usually means people who think that soup is food. People who can stand around with a glass of wine, talking about their job for two and a half hours without eating anything but small crackers with randomly placed bits of fish on them. They call it "hors d'oeuvres," but believe me, it's really nothing but a mystery novel about the mystery of where the hell they've hidden the real food.

The fact that I pre-eat before we spend

any time with these people has saved your mother and me from plenty of arguments. Like, for example, whether I "growled" or simply "cleared my throat demonstratively" at whoever it was who tried to reach for the potato chips when we were at our first couples dinner together and the hostess of the gathering casually mentioned that the dinner would be forty-five minutes late.

And, naturally, I've developed a number of particularly effective favorites for this pre-eating purpose. Like, for example, the pre-eating hot dog. It's two chorizo sausages, bacon, cheese, potato salad, béarnaise sauce, crispy onions, and some other good stuff in a full-size baguette. I'll eat that whenever we're going to a social event I'm particularly skeptical about. Often the kind where your mother, when I protest at having to wear a tie, reminds me that when we got married it was actually only until *my* death that she promised to love me for better and for worse.

I call it the L'Oréal Sausage. Because I'm worth it.

You start by taking a baguette and scooping out the middle with a long spoon. (You can keep the bread you scoop out. I usually roll it into balls and fry it in butter and beer while I'm making the hot dog, as a pre-pre-eating snack.) Then you fry the chorizo. Decide for yourself whether you want to use butter or oil. I use both. And then add a little extra butter. And then quite a lot of beer. Your mother isn't all that keen on me frying things in beer, so I sometimes make the hot dog over at your grandma and grandpa's instead. It's good to know, in that case, that this recipe calls for two cans of beer. Because your grandpa will want to drink one of them.

There can be a bit of smoke when you pour the beer into the pan, but don't worry about that. It is, as Zlatan Ibrahimović likes to say, "f-ing normal at this level of professional sports." I usually fry the sausages until they look like they've been beaten up by the characters in *Sons of Anarchy*. But if you don't watch all that much TV, you can probably take them out earlier if you like.

After that, you add the bacon. How high a temperature you fry it at is something you can decide for yourself. Personally, I like it when the pan is so hot that the bacon almost curls up in the fetal position and covers its eyes when you add it, but that's down to individual taste.

While the bacon rolls around in the pan, you can start filling the baguette with various good stuff. It's down to your own conscience what kind of good stuff you choose, but I like to start with mayonnaise and mustard. Don't be shy. It will not do you any good.

The mustard? I like it strong. Exactly how strong is, of course, up to you, but I like it when it's so strong that it starts screaming at you in an accent and suddenly marches away to pull a truck out of a ditch or defeat a Roman army. I think that's enough. Your grandpa has a pretty damn good homemade mustard that he makes by rolling a small cannonball around a plastic bowl full of mustard seeds. It's strong as hell. And if it's not strong enough, your grandpa sends angry letters to the local paper and threatens to report the mustard to various judicial and nonjudicial (and, in all honesty, often completely made-up) courts of law. That usually gets the mustard back in line.

People, of course, often ask why I need so much mayonnaise and mustard in the bread. But it's because the crispy onions just don't stick as well otherwise. This is important street-smart stuff for you, right there.

Next, I add melted cheese. If you want to, you can melt the cheese in the microwave, but I normally just use the cheese knife as a spatula for frying the sausage, and when the knife is covered in scalding-hot oil, I use it

195

to slice the cheese. Partly because it's effective, and partly because it makes me feel like it's what Rambo would do. Then I roll the cheese around the chorizo, and the bacon around the cheese. Like a cheese-and-bacon sleeping bag. After that, I push the chorizo/bacon/ cheese roll into the bread. If there's too much friction, you haven't used enough mayonnaise. No worries. There are only two things in life it's never too late for: an apology and more mayonnaise.

Next, you push all of your good stuff into the bread. You can choose whatever you want. I like potato salad, pickles, and crispy onions. Ideally so that the pickles are practically spooning the pieces of potato as they slip inside the baguette. Like the pickles and the potato were two freezing soldiers on a training exercise, promising each other never to talk about this with anyone.

If you feel like really spoiling yourself, you can add some kind of colorful garnish on top. We do actually eat with our eyes too. Some people like parsley and things like that, but I think that a little béarnaise sauce and some extra crispy onions look good. It's down to personal preference.

How many pre-eating hot dogs you eat before you leave is, of course, completely up to you. I normally eat three or four or so. But you only weigh about twenty pounds, so maybe one is enough for you.

And, well.

You're probably wondering what all this has to do with love, and I told you already. I don't know all that much about love. But your mother is a vegetarian. And she still chose me.

So I guess that might teach you more about this than anything else I can say.

Because the reason I don't know much about love is that I've really only ever loved one woman. But every day with her is like being a pirate in a magical land far away full of adventures and treasures. Making her laugh is a bit like wearing rain boots that are a little too big and jumping into the deepest of puddles.

I'm blunt and sharp and full of black and white. She's all my color.

But I don't think I complete her at all. I mostly cause trouble. And maybe that's the point, I don't know. But no one has ever, ever, ever said that we're perfect for one another. I'm a foot taller than she is and weigh more than twice as much. I have no sense of rhythm and my body balance is like a drunk panda's.

Your mother loves nothing in this life as much as she loves dancing, and she chose to share her time on Earth with a man she can't dance with without seriously fearing for her safety.

She chose me.

And then you came along. And you love music. And when you dance, you and she . . . If I could only choose one single moment to live inside for all eternity, it would be that.

I can't tell you anything about love. Nothing more than that.

THE EAGLE HAS NOT LANDED.

(*This morning*)

WIFE: Are you taking the car into town?

ME: Yeah.

WIFE: So can you drop him off at preschool?

ME: Yeah.

WIFE: Can you pick up the rug from the dry cleaner's too?

ME: Sure.

WIFE: And swing by the pharmacy? And do the food shopping on the way home?

ME: Yeah.

WIFE: Perfect. I'm going to work now, then. See you tonight!

(*Thirty minutes later*) . . .

ME: (*On the phone*) Hello?

WIFE: Hi! Did I remind you to pick up the rug from the dry cleaner's?

ME: Yeah.

WIFE: And that you need to swing by the pharmacy?

ME: Mmm.

WIFE: And that you sho—

ME: YEEES! Do you think I'm deaf or something?

WIFE: Nonono, sorry. I just wanted to check. You can be a bit forgetful sometimes, so I just wante—

ME: I'm not bloody SENILE!

WIFE: Nonono, sorry. See you tonight.

(*Another fifteen minutes later*)

WIFE: Hi, it's me again. Are you at the office?

ME: No, I'm in the car.

WIFE: Ah, okay. So everything was fine when you dropped him off at preschool this morning?

(*Fairly long silence*)

WIFE: Hello?

ME: (*Looking into the back seat, where our son is asleep in his car seat.*)

WIFE: Hel . . . lo?

ME: (*Clearing my throat*) All right. Hear me out, now. I know I can be slightly forgetful at times and I know I was rude to you this morning with the whole "I'm not senile" thing, but before you say anything now I just want you to remember that AT LEAST I'm not one of those parents who forgets to PICK UP my child from preschool . . .

This Seemed like a Slightly Less Idiotic and Irresponsible Idea at the Time.

But yes. Note to self: Wite-Out is really, really, really hard to get off a two-year-old.

■ ■ ■ ■

WHAT YOU NEED TO KNOW ABOUT WHEN I HOLD YOUR HAND A LITTLE TOO TIGHT

■ ■ ■ ■

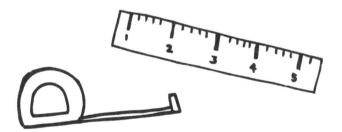

You're going to meet a lot of people in your life who'll try to tell you what the meaning of it all is. What we live for. Some of the brightest minds in world history have tried to sum it up. Musicians, authors, politicians, philosophers, artists, poets. They've talked about the transitory nature of life, about its irony, its passion, its desire, and its magic.

They've said and written grand, wonderful things.

I hope you get to read and hear all of them, because there's something so special in that experience, in falling in love with words. Feeling them like fluttering butterflies beneath your skin. Like whirlwinds in your head. Like a punch to the gut.

I've read the works of thinkers and prophets. The holy books, and the most unholy. I've benefited from mankind's most brilliant brains devoting entire lifetimes to explaining who we really are. What the hell we're doing here.

What life is all about.

But nothing has hit me as hard as this one line: "Life's a game of inches."

Al Pacino said that. In the locker room just before the final game in *Any Given Sunday.* Damn good film, that. There are people who will try to tell you that you need to love sports films or at least like football to be able to really appreciate it. But they've got it all wrong.

> "[L]ife's this game of inches. So is football. Because in either game, life or football, the margin for error is so small . . . One half a step too late or too early and you don't quite make it. One half second too slow or too fast, you don't quite catch it. The inches we need are everywhere around us. They are in every break of the game, every minute, every second. On this team, we fight for that inch."

There are people, and purely hypothetically we could call them "your mother," who will shake their heads and sigh so deeply that they need to pause halfway to take in more air every time I show you that film. But you and I know better.

Because life is all about the small margins.

A few inches here or there.

The job ad that took me to Stockholm might have been five inches. The stamp to get on the subway may be one. The threshold I stepped over at the very same moment I saw your mother for the first time might have been three. The first bed we slept in was about thirty-five.

Two birth cities can be two thousand miles apart. A first home can be two hundred square feet. A boy can be born and be nineteen inches.

A bullet can be 22 millimeters.

There's nothing from your childhood that I'll owe you a bigger apology for than always trying to impress you. So I guess I'll save this until you're old enough to think I'm so boring that I've probably never experienced anything exciting at all.

That's when I'll show you the scar and tell you about that day a few years before you were born.

And sure, in all honesty, you probably won't think I'm even an ounce cooler for it. But still. I'll take what I can.

The police said it was just an ordinary robbery. The kind that happens in banks and post offices and shops almost every day. "The important thing is that you realize this wasn't anything personal," they repeated over and over again. No one really knows exactly what happened. A couple of men with guns and another group of people in the wrong place at the wrong time, I guess, that's all. Like all robberies. Maybe the robbers got stressed out, maybe what happened next was more an accident than anything else. Hard to say.

But by the time they ran off, one of them had shot someone.

And I don't want to teach you to mouth off at the police or anything. But it's quite difficult to get shot and *not* "take it personally." Let's just leave it at that.

The bullet entered my thigh about four inches above my knee and burrowed through my flesh into my thighbone. Not that I knew that at the time, of course. One funny thing about being shot is that you don't really have time to perceive where you've been shot, when you are, in fact, shot. So it might have taken a second or two before I even realized that the gun had actually gone off, and that it'd been aimed at me. And then it took me another second to realize that it hadn't been aimed at my head.

People ask me all the time now whether I was afraid of dying. They say that your life is meant to flash before your eyes when it happens. And maybe it did for me too. But all I really remember is that the robbers had forced every one of us onto the floor, and then they took our cell phones and watches. And your mother had given me that watch for Christmas just a few weeks before.

We'd only been a couple for a few months, back then. And when the gun went off, I know that my first thought was that I might never see her again. And then I thought about what my father always said when I caused trouble as a child:

"What the hell, Fredrik, why does EVERY-THING always happen to YOU?!"

And then there were probably a few seconds there where I thought that if I did see your mother again, she would probably be all annoyed by the fact that I can't even be given a nice watch without going off and getting myself shot.

I'm hard to live with like that.

And people keep asking me if I was afraid of dying. But . . . no. And that's not because I'm especially macho or excessively brave or have an incredibly high pain threshold, but just because I kind of instinctively decided that this was probably one of those situations where it might be a good time to act like an adult. For once. "Survival instinct," biologists probably call it. "Good upbringing," if you ask your grandmother.

But me, I just thought that if I didn't lie completely still and keep quiet, the next bullet would probably end up in my neck. So I just lay there and kept my mouth shut. And when the robber raised the gun again, and fired it down into the floor, I thought that bullet had hit me too.

That's when I thought I would die.

My memories are a bit of a mess after that. But I heard sneakers running off. A door slamming shut. A car outside, tearing off. Worried voices shouting for me to lie still. I tried to get up anyway, of course, since I, well, you know. I'm kind of an idiot.

I remember my feet moving in thin air, and it was a bit like how I imagine cartoon characters feel in that second when they realize they've run over the edge of a cliff.

And then: the pain.

A pulsing merciless pain in my leg so massive that it consumed every ounce of my comprehension for what felt like a lifetime. As though someone were shooting me over and over and over again and again, only the bullets were coming from inside my body, out through my flesh, rather than the other way around.

I don't know how long I was lying on that floor. That pain is all I remember.

The next thing I recall is the police. Then the paramedics. I know that I started shouting at one of them because he said, "The helicopter's landed." Because I don't like flying. So I shouted something about how he could just bloody forget about getting me on that goddamn thing! And, well, as it turned out, he hadn't said anything about a helicopter at all. No one really knows where I got that from. Funny how the mind works.

And then they gave me enough drugs to make a racehorse sit down and drink a Dr Pepper and download Wordfeud on its phone.

From then on, all this really was much harder for your mother than it was for me. Being shot is actually the closest I've ever come to being a rock star. Everyone takes really good care of you.

Your mother, on the other hand, just got a phone call while she was at work, from someone saying I was on the way to the hospital. They weren't allowed to give her any details. Nothing about where I'd been shot, just that I had been, and that she needed to come in immediately. She had to jump into a taxi not knowing whether I would be alive or dead when she arrived. She had to contact my friends. She had to call my mom.

But me? I got morphine.

Not that I'm in any way encouraging you to take drugs, that is. I honestly only have very limited experience of them myself. There was that one incident when I was twenty, and I went to Thailand for a few months. I went to a party and fell asleep on a beach and woke up on a whole other island wearing a T-shirt someone had written WASABI on with a permanent marker. For the next two weeks, I had an insatiable craving for onion-flavor chips and tomato juice. And after that, I decided that this whole drug thing probably wasn't for me.

But morphine. Holy smoke, dude.

All I remember is that the nurses lifted me onto a stretcher and that I was singing. It's not altogether clear exactly what song, but I think it was "Afraid to Shoot Strangers" by Iron Maiden. And then I remember a nurse taking my hand and whispering gently that they needed to roll me onto one side and that I shouldn't be scared. I know I had time to wonder what the hell I had to be scared of now that I was in the hospital, unless she was planning on pulling a gun of her own. I think I even joked about it. She smiled the way salesclerks tend to smile when I tell a great story and they don't want to be rude. And then the nurses rolled me onto my side, and I felt four pairs of hands frantically searching my back. It wasn't until then that I realized there was so much blood on my clothes that they didn't know if there was more than one bullet wound.

And yes. At that point I got pretty goddamn scared.

But then they just gave me more morphine. And that fixed everything.

I know that while I was being wheeled into surgery, I told a nurse that she had to find my girlfriend and let her know I was fine and that everything would be okay. The nurse patted me on the head and told me not to worry about it. I immediately grabbed her wrist, fixed my eyes on her, and shouted, "You haven't met my girlfriend! I'm not saying this for my safety but for the safety of the staff at this hospital!" And then they gave me more morphine.

But I guess someone must have heard me and taken me seriously after all, because not long after, another nurse opened a door down in the waiting room, put a finger to her mouth for your mother to be quiet, and then nodded for her to follow. I think your mother must have been incredibly scared. I know she was crying. I guess I was safe in the eye of the storm while she was the one caught in the wind.

And I suppose there are very few people blessed enough to be able to tell you the exact second, down to the very moment, when they realized they wanted to wake up next to a particular person for the rest of their life.

Your mother always says that everything broke inside of her when the nurse, after leading her up and down stairs and along corridors, suddenly opened a door. And there I was, all covered in blood on a stretcher. I know that I turned my head and saw her and that I felt my heart in my fingertips. I'll remember that until I die. It was right there and then that I knew I would follow her to the ends of the Earth.

And . . . sure. Obviously I wish I could say that your mother felt all the same things at that exact moment. But, well, you know.

I was pretty stoned.

So what your mother saw, after running up and down stairs and along corridors with her heart in her throat and the tears streaming down her cheeks, was me lying on a stretcher, as far gone as a heavily sedated rhino, telling the nurses the joke about two Irishmen in a boat.

So right there and then, she was probably more tired of me than anything else. If we're being completely honest.

But she stayed. And aside from being half your gene pool, I'll always view the fact that I managed to make her do that as my top life achievement.

The doctors pulled the bullet out of my leg. Which really wasn't anywhere near as dramatic as it sounds. The real drama actually didn't happen until the next day, once all the drugs wore off and a nurse came in to take the catheter out of my . . . well, you'll learn as you get a bit older exactly where a catheter goes. And, seriously, if she'd given me the option of pulling it out or shooting me in the other leg right there and then, I probably would have needed a moment to ponder it.

And I was the lucky one in all this, it should be noted. The man in the bed next to me also had his catheter taken out that morning. But he had morning wood.

Anyway.

After that, they gave me a bottle of pills and told me I could go home. All in all, I wasn't even in the hospital for a day and a night. Bullet in, bullet out, and back in my own bed again before Jack Bauer had time to sort out a single episode of *24*.

Life is all about small margins. A few inches here and there.

The police showed me afterward which type of gun I'd been shot with. Showed me where I was lying on the floor and talked about how slightly different the angle of the weapon could have been. The shooter could have pointed it a little to the right, and maybe I would never have become a father. Slightly upward, and maybe I would never have walked again. A little farther upward, and, well, you know. I wouldn't be writing this.

I was on painkillers for a month. On crutches for two. Saw a psychologist for three. It took a spring for me to be able to walk properly again, a summer to learn to stop waking up in the middle of the night crying and screaming. And if you ever wonder why I always say that your mother is too good for me, there are ten thousand reasons.

But those nights are one of them.

She's a lion, your mother. Never forget that. Everyone took care of me, gave me pills and free taxi rides and beers in the local pub in exchange for me telling the story of how it felt to take a bullet. But it was your mother who held our lives together when I came tumbling down and crashed. She was the one who worked more than full-time and paid our bills and every morning and every night changed the bandage on a messy wound, which went as deep as a ballpoint pen into my thigh. She was the one who cheered like I'd scored the winning goal in a World Cup final when I called her at work just to say that I'd managed to climb into the bathtub all by myself for the first time. She was the one who held my hand and promised everything would be okay when I had to teach myself all over again to stand in line at the supermarket without having a panic attack.

She was the one who really took that bullet. Don't ever forget that.

That autumn, we went to Barcelona, and, in a small square by a small church, I got down on one knee and asked her never to get as annoyed at any other man for leaving wet towels on the floor as she does at me. The very next summer, we got married. And three weeks later, she woke me at dawn by hitting my forehead insanely hard with a plastic stick and shouting, "One line or two? DOYOUSEEONELINEORTWO???"

And the very next spring, you were born. Life's a game of inches.

So if we're ever standing by the gate at your school and I hold on to your hand just a little too tight. Or for a little too long. Then that's why. Most people never get to find out that they aren't immortal.

And I know I'll show the scar to you and your friends at some point in time, and when you walk away your friends will turn to you with wide eyes and say, "Seriously? Did he really get shot?" And then you'll allow a few dramatic seconds to pass. Stand up straight. Nod slowly and matter-of-factly. Look each of them straight in the eye. And then you'll shrug and say, "Nah, you know, my dad, he talks a lot. It's probably just a birthmark!"

I hope you won't be angry at me for still trying to impress you. I hope you won't hold this book against me.

You and your mother are my greatest, most wonderful, scariest adventure. I'm amazed every day that you're still letting me follow along.

So always remember: Whenever I'm difficult. Whenever I'm embarrassing. Unreasonable. Unfair. Just think back to that day when you refused to tell me where the hell you'd hidden my car keys.

And never forget that you started this.

ABOUT THE AUTHOR

Fredrik Backman is the author of the #1 *New York Times* best-seller *A Man Called Ove* (soon to be a major motion picture starring Tom Hanks), *My Grandmother Asked Me to Tell You She's Sorry, Britt-Marie Was Here, Beartown,* and *Us Against You,* as well as two novellas, *And Every Morning the Way Home Gets Longer and Longer* and *The Deal of a Lifetime.* He lives in Stockholm, Sweden, with his wife and two children.